COUPLES PARTING

COUPLES PARTING

How to Find the 'Good' in 'Goodbye'

TONY GOUGH

DARTON, LONGMAN AND TODD
London

First published in 1992 by
Darton, Longman and Todd Ltd
89 Lillie Road, London SW6 1UD

© 1992 Tony Gough

ISBN 0–232–51942–0

A catalogue record for this book is available
from the British Library

Phototypeset by Intype Ltd, London SW19 8DR
Printed and bound in Great Britain
at the University Press, Cambridge

To all those who facilitated my
growing and healing
and my discovery of a new and
joyful life –
my loving thanks

Contents

Preface

I am aware of some very mixed feelings on the completion
of this book. To begin with, it gives me some satisfaction
in completing the project of a quartet of books for couples
that first came to my mind while writing *Couples Arguing*
(1987). In that book I address the vital issues of communication between couples without which true and open
relationships are impossible. In *Couples in Counselling*
(1989) I tried to de-mystify the often threatening world of
counselling for those whose relationships run into trouble.
Couples Growing (1991) emphasized the more positive
aspects of marriage enrichment and how we can keep
marriages alive and growing. In *Couples Parting* a different
focus occupies my mind.

If there are positive advantages to be gained in learning
new ways of communicating in our marriage, in seeking
help if and when we need it to heal the wounds in our
marriage, and in finding ways in which to keep our
marriage healthy, could there be any similar positive
advantages when it comes to marriages that break up? Is
not the process of divorce analogous to death, and surely
there is nothing positive in death? As someone who has
been through the process of divorce I could not possibly
avoid these questions nor approach this subject dispassion-
ately.

It was at this point that I became aware of another set
of emotions. Could I bear to go back and unpack what
happened to me when my own marriage ended all those

years ago? Frankly it seemed to me that I really had no choice if I was to remain honest with myself and with my readers. But, if I shared some of my feelings, could I prevent my personal experiences from taking over? Would I simply wallow in self-pity? How could I hope to prevent the 'it-turned-out-OK-for-me-so-it-will-for-you' attitude seeping into what I wanted to share? I have wrestled painfully with these questions and you must judge for yourself how far I have managed to steer my way through the various temptations.

It is not by chance that the words 'guidelines' and 'guide' appear in the subtitles of my previous books.[1] The metaphor of the 'map' has certainly been central to my thinking. When I went to buy a map recently, prior to a holiday in France, I became aware that there are all sorts of maps. They seem to vary not just in size and price but also in scale. For example, the map that would see me through from Caen to Auray was little use in helping me to find the camp site we were heading for. I needed a different scale of map for that purpose. Once there, of course, there was yet a third map I needed to find my way around the streets of La Trinité sur Mer. So on what scale was I to base *Couples Parting*?

This is definitely not a street map. The environs of Gough City are totally unique, as are the circumstances surrounding each couple whose marriage breaks down. As Sam Keen reminds us: 'All maps of human life are composed of metaphors. To profit by one another's experiences, we must become adept at the art of playing with metaphor, translating images, listening for the meaning beneath the non-sense of just-so stories or myths.'[2] This book is therefore much more like a large-scale map which shows some contours of the terrain you can expect to pass through on your journey through separation and the death of a relationship. Just as a coach-load of people on the same outing will all return with different experiences and recollections of what they saw, people on the journey through separation – even the two people concerned – will recall different experiences and emotions. Whatever we partially *notice*, however, will always differ from the totality of what was *there*. As I have retraced my own journey through separation, I have struggled to stay honest with myself, while at the same time trying to gain a far deeper appreciation of what was going on than I was capable of at the time. By doing so, I hope I have not distorted my personal history, nor fallen into the trap of over-generalization.

In the 1960s there was a popular song that spoke for many people. It was 'Let's Hang On', sung by Frankie Valli and the Four Seasons. The opening lines go like this:

> There ain't no good in our goodbye:
> True love takes a lot of trying,
> Oh-oh, I'm crying.
>
> Let's hang on to what we've got.
> Don't let go, girl, we gotta lot
> Gotta lot of love between us,
> Hang on, hang on, hang on
> To what we've got.[3]

It takes a lot of energy to hang on to a dead or moribund marriage, while at the same time it hurts to let go. The unswerving belief I am left with is that, inherent in every one of our goodbyes, there *is* much 'good' that awaits our personal discovery. To that end I offer this final volume in the quartet, hoping you too will be able to find the 'good' in 'goodbye'.

TONY GOUGH
Western Park, Leicester

Acknowledgements

I would like to express my thanks to several people who directly helped me with the completion of this book. Mary Jean Pritchard, Editorial Director of Darton, Longman and Todd, has been a constant source of encouragement and hospitality when I deliver my typescripts to the office. Indeed, the whole staff at DLT have always shown care and courtesy in my dealings with them.

Next, I wish to thank the staff at the Tavistock Institute of Marital Studies in London. They have never failed to come to my rescue when I needed pointing in the direction of current research on modern marriage. I am especially grateful to Benita Dyal and Christopher Vincent for their mention of John C. Haskey's important paper referred to in Chapter 2. I am also grateful to my friend Kris Beuret who read an early draft of *Couples Parting* and for her helpful comments (also her kind permission for me to use her fax machine!).

There are many writers to whom I am indebted as part of my ongoing learning process and due acknowledgement is made in the text. Others, however, have become so much a part of me that I am unable to separate their contributions from my own. I am also mindful of the support and encouragement I received from many people during my own leavetaking process in 1980, and this book is dedicated to them. Though unnamed, they will know who they are and, hereby, how grateful to them I remain to this day.

Endings are, let's remember, experiences of dying. They are ordeals, and sometimes they challenge so basically our sense of who we are that we believe they will be the end of *us*. This is where an understanding of endings and some familiarity with the old passage rituals can be helpful. For as Mircea Eliade, one of the greatest students of these rituals, has written: 'In no rite or myth do we find the initiatory death as something *final*, but always as the condition *sine qua non* of a transition to another mode of being, a trial indispensable to regeneration; that is, to the beginning of a new life.' (William Bridges, *Transitions*)[4]

1. Moving Out – Moving In – Moving On

We are Siamese twins.
  Our blood's not sure
   if it can circulate,
  now we are cut apart.
Something in each of us is waiting
  to see if we can survive,
    severed.

(Denise Levertov, 'Divorcing')

Saturday, 19 January 1980. Moving day had finally arrived. I have memories of loading up my car and the hired van and making the short journey from Leicester to Rugby several times.

The final pieces of my belongings were unloaded and the last of my helpers were leaving, taking with them the van. A voice said to me, 'It's not the end of the world!' But that's just how it felt. I closed the door behind them. I imagined I could hear an echo of a number of other doors I was closing at the same time: my marriage, my vocation, my stable way of life, my respectability, my pastoral responsibility. I was utterly alone.

It was around midnight. I made my way up the thirty-two stairs to the small attic flat, every stair trodden with heaviness and an almost paralysing sense of aloneness. I stared vacantly at the teachests full of books and my bits of furniture. The chaos of moving was evident all around me. This outer chaos was but an extension, a symbol, of my inner turmoil. My ordered world had collapsed. As Sam Keen discovered on his personal journey (and relates movingly in *To a Dancing God*), everything that was nailed down suddenly came loose: 'Chaos was king and the moral world looked like a furniture store after the hurricane.'[5] I knew what he meant as I gazed around me. No one told me how alone I would feel, and how easily panic could rise from the depths like a tidal wave threatening to overwhelm and destroy either me or my sanity. After nearly twenty-six years of marriage, we finally had to call it a day. I had nothing more to give, either to my marriage or my parish; I was burnt out. The strain of living together became too much and we agreed upon a trial separation. Truth to tell, the separation had started much earlier – the slow, imperceptible growing apart. Yet the pain of maintaining the façade of living together had concealed a greater pain that was to come.

That cold January night almost every fibre of my being wanted to go back. I was terrified I wouldn't last the night. I ached with a longing, born of panic, to be back home: only there was no 'home' for me there any longer. I tried desperately to recall all the good reasons for leaving in the first place; there now appeared a huge gulf between the idea and the reality. The strain of trying to support a collapsing marriage had masked the full consequences of separation. How would I survive in this wilderness? The twin forces of my fear and my integrity raged in combat. I felt like a battle-ground, a boxing-ring in which two fighters were slugging it out to the death.

That night was not the moment for working out neat answers to the conflict when I hardly knew what the questions were. Exhausted, I crashed into bed, trying to leave the questions behind. Sleep was fitful, full of wild, forgotten dreams.

I awoke to the ringing of church bells. Sunday! Bloody Sunday! I began to laugh at the irony of it – a priest lying in bed on a Sunday morning! Perhaps only those who have had their lives governed by bells and the times of church services for twenty years, like some latter-day Pavlovian dog, may be able to appreciate the joke. Like a madman I shouted at the bells, 'Ring for all you're worth! *I'm not coming!*' I had more important things to do. I found the kettle and made some tea, and went back to bed. It was the first day of a strange and eerie new world. This was Rugby, January 1980. A new decade. This was my transit camp. I recalled how much it felt like being evacuated during the war. Sitting on the floor of a school classroom in Kettering with a luggage label on my jacket. I waited for someone to claim me. I watched longingly as one by one the children in my group were chosen by the fostering parents. I was the last child to be chosen. Today no one was coming, no matter how long I waited.

I sipped my tea, and cautiously began to recreate the world.

For such a momentous and frightening task, I had no map, no blueprint. I had an ache in my heart (chest pains were to be my daily companion for almost a year), a sense of having done all that I could to make the departure from my last pastoral charge less of a rout and more of an orderly withdrawal, and a fragile hope in my growing personal integrity and of a more satisfying future. Where? How? With whom? I had no idea whatever. I only knew that I had to get through this transition on my own. Contrary to the fairly predictable and malicious diocesan gossip, there was no lover in whose arms I could find the anaesthetic for my pain and some instant comfort and acceptance. In addition to my personal inner pain, I also had to contend with the external painful wounds from what Harry Williams calls 'the consecrated claw'.

There was no question that my feelings of rejection increased my sense of depression. I had just suffered the biggest and most painful rejection of my whole life. I had surrendered all the important roles through which I had identified my self for almost thirty years. I felt like a bottle that had many role-labels attached to it. As these labels peeled off, one by one, with shock and a growing sense of terror, I found *there was no bottle there!* I felt for the first time a sense of existential terror which, had I been able to verbalize it at all, would have sounded like, 'Am I here? Do I exist?' I once described my feelings to a friend: 'It's a bit like being born and raised in a forest, and waking up one day to find all the trees gone!' Utter disorientation. Suicidal thoughts surfaced for the first time in my life.

My new world included a number of contradictions. The anonymity of Rugby was bliss. I could walk through the streets without having to put on my 'nice vicar' face. I could scowl if I wanted to. I knew no one. No one knew me. I felt free. Yet there was a price to pay for this freedom. There was no one to talk to. No one would know if I lived or died. I found myself staring brazenly into warmly-lit living rooms, watching families have tea around the TV – and resenting them all bitterly!

I could lie in bed as long as I liked. Bliss! Yet – supposing I lost the *will* to get up and just mouldered? That possibility sharpened my mind. I needed a map! I needed some self-imposed routine that would get me through each day with my mind intact. I resolved:

Up by 9 a.m. latest
Have breakfast – wash up
Clean the flat – even though it was spotless

Go shopping – don't forget *The Times* and a cream
cake for tea
Have coffee
Read *half* the newspaper, but leave the crossword for
later
Prepare lunch – have lunch – wash up
Plan an afternoon visit: shops, swimming or a jog
Have a shower
Make tea
Wash up
Telephone someone – *anyone*
Finish the crossword
Listen to records (I had no TV) or read
Bed – but never before 10 p.m.

This routine probably saved my sanity. As banal as it may
sound, I organized it *in order to establish my existence.*
It was not just the isolation I was feeling and fighting. It
was a whole catalogue of things that happened to coincide,
so that the whole of my feelings was more than the sum
of their parts: depression, anger, resentment, an over-
whelming sadness, longing, determination, relief – all
these jangled within me, though I often hadn't the faintest
idea who 'me' was. I felt lost.

C. S. Lewis began his own exploration of grief with
these words: 'No one ever told me that grief felt so like
fear. I am not afraid, but the sensation is like being afraid.'[6]
I was often far weaker than that; I *was* afraid. I was not
aware of it at the time but I was suffering from multiple
grief.

With my feelings of loss came other experiences, like
doubt. The tantalizing questions, usually beginning with
that threatening, insidious word *supposing*, began to haunt
my mind. I do not think I had ever felt the corrosive effect
of that word until then. Doubt began to intrude into my

every thought. Supposing this separation did not work? (How would I know if it had 'worked' anyway?) Supposing I couldn't hold out on my own? What then? Supposing I couldn't get a job before my planned course of study in the United States? Supposing I didn't get the fellowship in Chicago I had applied for? And so on.

But it was not only doubt that I had to contend with. Childhood terror returned with a vengeance. All my old feelings of insecurity, inferiority and abandonment – like those of evacuation – returned to form part of my daily experience. I felt no one cared a damn whether I lived or died, doubtless a projection of my inner sense of desperation and self-hatred. I felt sorry for myself. I was angry with everyone, especially the God I had served faithfully for thirty years. Religiously there was a cosmic gap which, while threatening, did at least mean that I could abandon my religious commitment. Since God had buggered off – two could play at that game! I began playing the other time-honoured game of 'Why should this happen to me?' until eventually my sense of humour surfaced and I could laugh at my own stupidity.

Humour has always been an important part of my life, and I recall while wandering around a bookshop I came across Woody Allen's book, *Without Feathers*.[7] If I don't actually owe my life to that book I most certainly owe to it a sense of perspective on my problems at that time. I read it with tears – of laughter this time – streaming down my face.

On other occasions, my tears were those of utter desolation and isolation. Why had partings to feel like this? Does leavetaking always have to be so painful? Is it just something I had to learn to live with, and live *through*? Would it ever stop hurting?

These are some of the questions I wrestled with daily. The poet Rainer Maria Rilke once wrote: 'be patient

toward all that is unsolved in your heart and . . . try to
love the *questions themselves . . . Live* the questions now.'[8]
At times my patience ran pretty thin; I felt in a constant
rage.

What was happening to me? I could not fully understand
it at the time but I was in a massive transition from a way
of life that was secure and familiar to one of utter isolation
and unfamiliarity. In spite of my counselling training (*I
ought to have known* said a know-it-all parent voice within
me), I was little prepared for the shock of it all. What
I was experiencing was, of course, what many people
experience when they separate from their partners: a mixture of confusion, anger, hurt, loneliness, and – worse still
– financial ruin. It helped me to understand why so many
broken marriages precariously survive. The partners are
held together by a glue made up of mutual panic and a
paralysing fear of what would become of them were they
to separate.

Looking back on those painful days in Rugby I feel
enormously proud of what I managed to achieve in spite
of the bleak prospects before me. I had to relearn my
survival skills. I recall painting the flat to give me something to do, listening to Radio 2 and the love-songs that
seemed to dominate the programme. There seemed to
be broken hearts everywhere! I am also grateful beyond
measure to the few people I knew who did not abandon
me. Most people find it impossible to maintain an even-
handed friendship with both parties in a broken relationship. They usually decide to distance themselves from
both. Of many colleagues in the clergy, only three made
contact with me and two of those have never spoken to
me since. Visitors to my flat were literally a godsend. I
believe I owe my sanity to their care and understanding.
I have dedicated this book to them.

I ask myself, 'If someone had given me *Couples Parting*

at that time, would I have found it helpful? I honestly believe I would, for this reason. In September 1980, when I eventually arrived in the United States of America for postgraduate studies, a student lent me *Going Home* by Robert A. Raines, which I read on my second night in Chicago. In an uncanny way Robert Raines appeared to be relating my own story, as he unfolded what had happened to him when he left his parish ministry and his twenty-five-year-old marriage. He writes about a recurring image that flashed across his mind concerning the guilt he felt about leaving his wife:

> Peg [his wife] and I were in a deer park; I was the warden, and she was the helpless and defenceless deer. I, the warden, whose job it was to protect the deer from harm, to take care of it, instead turned and shot the deer between the eyes. Later, as I described this image to a counsellor, he suggested I revise the image so that instead of shooting the deer between the eyes, I see myself as the warden opening the gate of the park so that the deer would now be free to go out and find her own life, free of being fenced in and confined by me, the warden. (Years later, Peg told me that is exactly what had happened.)[9]

I remember reading the first chapter and beginning to cry uncontrollably. 'Thank God!' was all I could repeat to myself, 'Thank God this has all happened to someone like me, and he has survived!' I place on record my gratitude to Robert Raines for giving me (and others) permission to enter into his own suffering when I needed something to hang on to. He had been there, and had come through. Perhaps I could, too.

It is in the hope that this book may reach you at your point of need that I dare to uncover my personal pain. Of course, your story and my story are unique to each of us.

I respect that. Yet, remembering how much I was helped by *Going Home* and other stories of human beings in pain, I am hopeful that in its turn my story may be an encouragement to you too. By *living the questions* you can come through to a new life. As Robert Raines says, 'It is not having the answers, but being driven and drawn by questions . . . Faith requires us to learn to trust the process.'[10] Of course, all growing involves some experience of pain but this book is written with the unswerving conviction that at least this can be a creative experience. It is not enough just to move out and to move in. We also need to move on.

2. Some Reasons Why Couples Separate

> Why should such a foolish Marriage Vow
>   Which long ago was made,
> Oblige us to each other now
>   When Passion is decay'd?
> We lov'd, and we lov'd, as long as we cou'd,
>   Till our Love was lov'd out in us both:
> But our Marriage is dead, when the Passion is fled:
>   T'was Pleasure first made it an Oath.
>   (John Dryden, from *Marriage à la Mode*, 1672)

Why do couples separate? This apparently obvious, and necessary, question does not allow us the luxury of any obvious single answer. While it would be incorrect to say that there are as many reasons as there are couples, such a response would at least alert us to the complexity implicit within the question. Neither can the question be separated from the deeper, underlying issue as to why the couple married the first place.

As a starting point perhaps it would be helpful to suggest that there are two important issues to focus on in the separation of couples. First there are the legal grounds which describe the mechanics of the separation process and which are available to statistical study from the judicial records. Secondly there are the psychological and behavioural reasons that bear upon the uniqueness of the relationship of individual couples. I will call these two parts of the answer the *grounds* of separation and the *background* to separation.

THE GROUNDS OF SEPARATION[11]

The 1969 Divorce Reform Act introduced a solitary ground for divorce, which was the 'irretrievable breakdown of marriage'. Under the Act (with its subsequent revisions) a petitioner for divorce has to prove one of five facts:

1. *Adultery:* the petitioner has to prove that their spouse has committed adultery and that the petitioner finds this person now intolerable to live with;
2. *Behaviour:* the petitioner must prove that their spouse has behaved in such a way that they cannot reasonably be expected to continue to live with them;
3. *Desertion:* the petitioner must prove that their partner has deserted them for a period of at least two years;
4. *Two Years' Separation:* the parties to the marriage must have lived apart for a continuous period of at least two years immediately preceding the presentation of their petition, and both spouses consent to the decree being granted;
5. *Five Years' Separation:* the parties to the marriage must have lived apart for a continuous period of at least five years immediately prior to the presentation of the petition.

It is within this judicial framework that we find the

grounds for divorce. By a careful analysis of the figures available some interesting data emerge. For example, in 1981 145,713 divorce petitions were granted and the average length of the marriages dissolved was 10.1 years. These figures however represent marriages that lasted an average of five years (petitions granted to wives after two years' separation where no children were involved) to an average of twenty-seven years (petitions granted to wives after five years' separation where there were no dependent children). For husbands in social class I (professional) the average duration of marriage was just under twelve years, whereas for those in social class V (unskilled) it was 8.4 years. It is no surprise to discover that couples with children tend to remain together twice as long as couples without children. The picture that emerges is consistent throughout the period 1961–88, that the majority of marriages dissolved were of five to nine years' duration. The average age at divorce is 35.8 years for men, and 33.4 years for women. The distribution of divorce petitions was 42,085 granted to husbands and 102,170 granted to wives. (The 1988 figures were consistent with this proportion: 49,000 granted to men and 134,000 granted to women.) Men are therefore almost three times as likely to be divorced by their spouses than women.

This imbalance of almost 3:1 in favour of women is seen in the facts alleged for the grounds for divorce. They also make interesting, though not surprising, reading. While men divorcing their wives for adultery (the most frequent reason cited by men), accounted for only 18.3 per cent, women divorcing their husbands for adultery accounted for 25.6 per cent. And while men divorcing their wives for unreasonable behaviour accounted for only 4.3 per cent, this increased to 44.4 per cent in the case of wives divorcing their husbands (the most likely reason cited by wives' petitions). The figures would suggest that men are more likely to be divorced for unreasonable behaviour than for adultery, while women are more likely to be divorced because of adultery than for unreasonable behaviour.

The figures also show which marriages are most at risk. For instance, men in the armed forces are more likely to divorce their wives for adultery (64 per cent) than the other way round (24 per cent). While wives of 'economically inactive' husbands obtain divorces accounting for 46 per cent, this rises to 67 per cent in the case of husbands described as 'unskilled'. The figure for husbands who are unemployed accounted for 57 per cent. We are seeing here some of the influences of the social conditions in Great Britain impacting upon divorce figures. The figures appear to be consistent however: men are more likely to be divorced because of unreasonable behaviour than adultery; women are more likely to be divorced because of adultery than unreasonable behaviour.

These are the bare legal statistics concerning the grounds for divorce. They indicate in a quite predictable way the factors that enhance the chances of a marriage failing. These factors are both social (the 'social class' of the respondent) and behavioural. What of the other, less easily defined reasons that concern the psychological make-up of the couples concerned? We turn now to the backgrounds of the divorcing couples.

THE BACKGROUND TO SEPARATION

Behind each of the grounds for divorce noted above lies a complicated background that has played an important – though occasionally invisible – role in the prelude to separation. Backgrounds are often taken for granted. 'Background music' may not be given our attention but it forms part of our environment. Similarly, each of us brings our own personal background into our marriage and many of us have learned to take it for granted. But it is within our experience of childhood, and particularly of adolescence, that patterns have been established in terms of how we form – or fail to form – creative relationships.

All our early experience of life we therefore bring into our marriage. Some of us bring creative models of human relationships while others bring destructive models. Until we become aware of our own patterns of establishing and maintaining personal relationships we may find ourselves merely repeating, albeit unconsciously, patterns we learned in our past that may have caused us great pain. Acts as well as attitudes are often brought lock, stock and barrel into a marriage, where they can create havoc.

In his helpful study, *Marital Breakdown*, Jack Dominian suggests three personality traits which most frequently contribute to marital breakdown and it will be useful to examine them at this point. He defines these as dependency, deprivation and lack of self-esteem.

Dependency

This is the condition into which every baby is born. Unlike others in the animal kingdom, humans are utterly incapable of doing anything for themselves at birth and therefore rely totally on the nurture and care by others for their survival. The needs of the newborn are at first physical – food, warmth, gentle touch and a friendly, secure environment. But there are other, psychological needs the baby has: love, caring, bonding to mother and parent-figures. When these needs – both physical and psychological – are met adequately, we are then more able to trust our environment and eventually to move outwards towards independence and maturity and mutually satisfying relationships. However, serious problems arise when such natural development is thwarted. Dr Dominian warns, 'The failure to achieve a minimum of emotional independence is one of the main causes of marital breakdown.'[12]

This emotional independence is a mark of adult maturity. We are no longer a helpless child dependent upon others but can make appropriate choices by ourselves. We can ask for things, we can co-operate with others in achieving identified aims and objectives.

However, there are thousands of people who get married with their childhood need for dependence still intact. They expect their partner to meet all their physical and emotional needs and of course they are often disappointed. Many then simply look elsewhere for more adequate 'parenting'. Such behaviour is childish; appropriate to a helpless and vulnerable child but out of place in an adult lifestyle. Perhaps the grounds for divorce already mentioned make sense at this point: whereas men will traditionally begin to act unreasonably, with or without physical violence, women will have affairs. This is where the grounds and backgrounds to divorce coincide. Many people are merely acting out their childhood pattern of dependent behaviour rather than choosing the more painful yet necessary task of growing up. Since many are ignorant of the ways of achieving adult maturity, they regress to their old and well-worn childhood pattern of getting their needs met.

Others will experience in their partners an over-dependence and clinging which, to begin with, may help to create a sense of 'being needed'. We feel like the 'strong one' and gain satisfaction from showing our partner that we are capable of meeting their emotional needs. However, this does not always last for ever. Such marriages can degenerate into the 'Peter Pan and Wendy' syndrome where wife becomes 'mother' or husband becomes 'father'; the partner agrees to play the part of the child.

Sooner or later the game is played out and 'mother' or 'father' wish for an adult relationship with their spouse and for them to learn to stand on their own two feet. The feelings of total responsibility for the marital relationship by 'mother' or 'father' prove too much and they begin to long for a relationship with a fully-developed adult rather than a baby. (The widespread use of apparently innocent and even attractive 'baby-talk' for adult partnerships should alert us to this danger.) At this point the unreasonable behaviour or adultery usually begins to surface and we can now see clearly the roots of this kind of behaviour.

Most couples find a certain degree of dependence on their partners an appropriate expectation. We usually work at the relationship out of our individual strengths, and many couples have evolved a pattern of division of labour and expectations that accomplishes this without too much trouble. If he loves cooking and she hates it, or he hates ironing and she loves it, both cooking and ironing can be taken care of in an atmosphere free from recriminations and too much exploitation. Interdependence is a cornerstone of growing marriages. This is a far cry from the abject dependence shown in many marriages, which palls with the passing of time.

Unfortunately the 'passive/dominant' model of relating is a widespread feature among couples, though there are rewards to be found in both of these positions. The passive partner can happily abandon every vestige of responsibility ('playing weak'), while the dominant partner can wield all the power and make the decisions ('playing strong'). This classic top-dog, under-dog model has within it, however, a hidden agenda: the under-dog usually wins! Playing upon their (implicitly agreed) weakness, the under-dogs can pull all the strings and, in effect, retain the power at the same time. It is a variation of the dependency theme in so far as it soon becomes a relationship based on co-dependency; they need each other in order to play the game.

Deprivation

Modern research has shown fairly conclusively that most of us arrive at the age of majority with our childhood wounds unhealed. One of these wounds is undoubtedly the issue we have been discussing – dependence upon others. Related to this, however, is the key issue of deprivation: the absence or lack of experiences that are vital to the development of a physically and psychologically healthy person. Whether in the realms of touch, warmth, food, security, a sense of worth or a need for acceptance and approval, many of us have been deprived. This is not always brought about by fiendish parents who abuse their children; the mere repetition by parents of 'how things were done when I was a child' may be enough to deprive the subsequent generation of vital resources of being and well-being.

What happens, then, to all those unmet needs from our childhood? They get stored in our unconscious mind where they await suitable opportunities to sneak out and get satisfied. To search for a partner who will fulfil all those things of which we felt deprived when a child is the most natural thing in the world. It is upon this shaky basis that countless marriages are founded. Our unconscious needs form part of what Harville Hendrix and others now call the 'unconscious marriage', the search for someone who will heal our childhood wounds of deprivation. Hendrix says, 'You fell in love because your . . . brain believed that it had finally found the ideal candidate to make up for the psychological and emotional damage you experienced in childhood.'[13]

It becomes obvious that in most of these unconscious

searches we fail abysmally. Our hopes of an all-sustaining mother or all-providing father are short-lived. We recoil in disillusion and disappointment. We experience feelings of having been let down or cheated. 'But you said you'd always look after me,' the husband quotes correctly. Yet did the wife really know what she was taking on? Neither husband nor wife actually knew of the hidden element of deprivation buried deeply within the man. Or, they may have 'known' with their heads in terms of his history but failed to appreciate the implications in the here-and-now marriage. Very often, in matrimonial rows, quite accurate accusations applicable to this theme are thrown around: 'Oh, grow up, for God's sake!' 'You're acting like a spoilt child!' 'It's time you learned to stand on your own two feet!' 'I can't be responsible for meeting all your expectations!'

Childhood deprivation wreaks untold havoc in marriages. As Alexander Pope wrote in his *Moral Essays*, 'Just as the twig is bent the tree's inclined.'

Lack of self-esteem

Jack Dominian writes: 'Complete or partial rejection of self as inferior, bad, and unworthy of love completes the triad of the significant traits in personality which contributes to marital breakdown.'[14] It is not difficult to understand why this should be the case.

Our feelings about ourself are brought into the partnership of marriage and are crucial for determining its success. The origins of our adult feelings about ourselves are carved out of the raw material of our childhood experiences. Those of us who had good and nurturing parents who helped us to distinguish between our Being (who I am) and our Doing (what I do) will be more adequately prepared for a lifetime of sharing and caring with others. It is essential for a child to be given a sense of its *unconditional goodness* as a basis for all future development. Unfortunately most of us are given a conditional sense of our goodness, that is, we are acceptable and accepted only if we conform to certain norms within our family. The key word is 'if': 'If you pass your exams . . . If you're a good boy/girl . . . If you please me . . . If you do as I tell you . . .' The message we receive (whatever message is intended) is, 'Your goodness is dependent on doing as others tell you.' Of course, our behaviour will not always please other people. We will do things that are wrong or naughty, but it is vital that parents distinguish between their child's essential goodness (their Being) and their naughty or unacceptable behaviour (their Doing). Most children are given a sense of 'badness' which they understand in an absolute way: 'I am bad!' It is quite possible – and desirable – that we can love the child while at the same time disapprove of their behaviour. 'I like you, Sam, but I don't like what you're doing' is a creative and logical response.

To those who bring their childhood sense of 'badness' with them intact into their marriage there are certain predictable things that can be said. They are going to reflect in the marriage the image of the bad self that they were given in childhood. It can emerge as a crippling sense of inferiority: 'I have a wonderful wife/husband who loves me and three super kids, but I feel I don't deserve them!' Their sense of inferiority is carried like a burden, never able to accept a compliment, never believing that they deserve anything good. They can emerge as family doormats, or walking apologies, or the Ugly Duckling of the family. That is bad enough, but there is worse yet. Such people will be looking to their partners to make them feel better while at the same time being unwilling to change their negative attitude towards themselves! It is a Catch-

22 situation: 'My world is broken! Mend it – only I won't let you.' The epitaph engraved on my previous marriage was precisely that: 'You must – but I won't let you!' It was a hopeless situation, to be trapped between a terrifying need and the implacable defences that prevented me from meeting it. No matter how much love and care was poured into the marriage, it simply ran out the other side. Nothing was ever enough. Jack Dominian correctly summarizes this situation:

> An acceptance of self as a person capable of love and worthy to receive it, free from exaggerated feelings of inadequacy or destructiveness and hostility, are the essential characteristics of self-esteem and essential requirements for an enduring relationship. In the extreme form of self-denigration spouses are unable to accept, or retain the care and affection offered from others. These men and women live with the certain conviction of their badness. Desperately anxious to be accepted and loved, they go on reacting to the positive response of others, as if it was not meant for them, or if inescapably directed towards them, it is outwardly accepted and inwardly refused *as it meets with their own rejection of themselves.*[15]

Such issues concerning self-esteem are frequently raised in the context of marital counselling, and it is clear to me that they represent one of the major predisposing causes to marital breakdown.

Dependency, deprivation and lack of self-esteem are three major features in the background to many divorces. To isolate three factors is, of course, simplistic yet it illustrates how hidden elements in our childhood backgrounds can surface within our marriage and wreck them. They are at least sufficient to help us in our understanding of the legal grounds of divorce: adultery, unreasonable behaviour and separating from our partners. They do not account for all the hidden psychological reasons for marital breakdown, but they cover much of the background to couples parting. Sexual difficulties, frequently quoted as a reason for marital breakdown, are often found to be symptoms of a deeper issue. Adultery is as likely to be the result of marital deprivation as indicative of being over-sexed. It may not condone the act but it helps to set it in a context of pain. Take, for example, the case of Meg and Rex.

Case history: Meg and Rex

Their marriage was basically happy, but Rex suffered from premature ejaculation. He was deeply embarrassed by this condition but too proud to seek sexual therapy in which, if not the result of some organic malfunction, it could have been easily and swiftly dealt with. Meanwhile Meg was left with her sexual feelings deeply unsatisfied. That she should respond to a caring relationship at work ending in a sexual affair, while not 'right' in everyone's eyes, in the circumstances could be at least understood. What is Meg to do? Go on suffering in silence in the face of Rex's refusal to seek help; or seek (or respond to if not positively sought after) a caring sexual relationship with someone else? This is an agonizing situation to be in, as many frustrated wives have related to me in counselling. Where the woman is a practising Christian – worse still, when she is the vicar's wife – the situation is well-nigh intolerable.

One husband's cri de coeur

Other couples, while not suffering from this particular problem, may have different sexual complaints, like the man who wrote the following letter to his wife:

> To my ever-loving wife
> During the past year I have attempted to seduce you 365 times. I succeeded thirty-six times. This averaged once every ten days, the following is a list of excuses made on the unsuccessful occasions:

We will wake the children	7	The baby is crying	18
It's too hot	15	Watched late show	7
It's too cold	3	Watched early show	5
Too tired	19	Mudpack on	12
It's too late	16	Grease on face	6
It's too early	9	Reading Sunday paper	10
Pretending to sleep	33	You are too drunk	9
Windows open, neighbours will hear	3	We have company in the next room	7
Your back ached	16	Your parents were staying with us	5
Toothache	2	My parents were staying with us	5
Headache	26		
Giggling fit	2		
I've had too much	4	Is that all you ever think about?	105
Not in the mood	21		

> Do you think you could improve our record this coming year?
>   Your ever-loving husband.[16]

While this 'letter' is clearly a spoof (and such a negative reaction is by no means an exclusively feminine characteristic), it does make clear the kind of difficulties that couples may experience within their relationship. Moreover it is not difficult to see how they can be expressed in the marriage alongside some of the other factors mentioned earlier.

All of these factors represent the background against which we can make a start in understanding why couples separate. Somewhere along the process of the marriage one of the parties either brings things to a head by talking about their problems, or – more probably – they begin *to act out* their reaction to the problems. Either way, it can lead to separation. Sometimes, for example where the talking leads to a period of short-term marriage counselling, the problem may be resolved and a more constructive way forward can be discovered and pursued. Unhappily, however, this is not always possible.

THE BREAKDOWN OF THE RELATIONSHIP

As a result of the frustration experienced because of the destructive factors mentioned earlier, the relationship inevitably begins to deteriorate. It really does take 'two to tango' and, while it is not impossible for a marriage relationship to be kept going on the energies of just one of the partners, the strain tells in the end. It is rather like trying to build a bridge over a river from one side. It doesn't work. This is no disrespect to the gallant efforts of the person in the relationship who is trying to keep it going single-handed. Herculean efforts are often made, compromises sought, concessions made beyond what may be thought reasonable; turning a blind eye to the aggravation experienced, biting one's tongue when tempted to lash out verbally, even enduring humiliation and provocation from the spouse; all these are frequently resorted to and generally to no avail. It is not for want of trying that they finally get the message: this marriage is dead.

Many people attempt to fend off that awful truth by playing mind-games with themselves. 'If I give him more time . . . Maybe it's not as bad as I imagine . . . She's just going through a phase . . . Think of the children . . . He's always come back to me in the past . . . It's probably my fault . . .' The attempts to rationalize the deteriorating marriage are almost infinite. Usually, as a last resort, some couples may seek the help of counselling agencies such as RELATE but it is often found that the condition of the marriage has deteriorated so far that any remedial work is found to be impossible. The best that can be done in those circumstances is to facilitate a constructive way out of the marriage.

Failure?

Many people are haunted by the fear of failure. There is usually a long history of this fear carried within most of us, and from time to time the thought of adding to the catalogue of our failures is daunting. We begin to see our marriage falling about our ears, and as if that were not enough to cope with we add to our misery the fear of failing other people. We start to ask, 'What will we tell the children . . . my mother and father . . . my sister who always envied my marriage . . . the neighbours . . . the vicar . . . my colleagues at work?'

The 'what-will-so-and-so-say?' factor keeps a lot of marriages functioning long after their 'sell-by date'. The advantages, of course, are not hard to find. It means that we can fend off those awkward questions from relatives and friends a little longer. We can also indulge in our wishful thinking that it will turn out all right in the end. It is at this point that we can identify one of the major stresses in marital breakdown: the bottling up of unwelcome thoughts and feelings.

It takes an enormous amount of energy to keep such

thoughts and feelings hidden and denied, and it is frequently found to be a major contribution to depression and other physical disorders. Worry and anxiety will emerge eventually, one way or another. This in turn makes us less able to deal with the marital crisis since most of our energy is being absorbed in the denial process; and so the vicious spiral goes on, deeper and deeper, with us right in the middle. Small wonder that thoughts of suicide frequently occur at this stage. The question naturally arises: is this really better than admitting the truth to ourselves, even if 'failure' has to be faced? The writer A. Alvarez correctly assesses the difference between divorce and suicide: 'Divorce and suicide have many characteristics in common and one crucial difference: although both are devastatingly public admissions of failure, divorce, unlike suicide, has to be lived through.'[17]

Admitting this to ourselves may be one thing; admitting it to other people is another. The degree of difficulty will be partly determined by who the significant 'other people' are. Our children, especially when they are very young, are the ones we often have the most difficulty with, and I would recommend some of the books available on this specific issue (see Further Reading, p. 126). Our inner family circle will be a large determining factor in what, if any, support we are given. Clearly families differ widely in their reaction to marital failure, particularly where a 'stiff-upper-lip' attitude prevails and where the motto is 'We don't have divorces in our family'. Our own royal family has had to bite some rather hard bullets in regard to the divorce of Princess Margaret and the separation of the Princess Royal and Captain Mark Phillips. (Public reaction to these and other events in the royal family reflected in a Gallup Poll in July 1991 showed that a majority of 51 per cent disagreed that 'The royal family provides a good example of family life'. In the case of those under twenty-five years of age, the figure was 75 per cent.)

Some people will receive the news of the actual or impending separation with a sense of shock. Some of us have skilful ways of keeping the cracks of our disintegrating marriage concealed but we cannot shield ourselves from their reactions when they are expressed directly to us. I recall a GP ringing me up and lecturing me about the Christian doctrine of marriage and its indissolubility, and saying shouldn't I be ashamed of myself, especially as a member of the clergy, and so on. Some people will express their sense of shock verbally; others will take more deviant measures such as indulging in the game of 'ain't it awful' among themselves or – by far the most hurtful way – ignoring us altogether. I found their silence inexplicable and, while with hindsight I can fully understand their not knowing what to say, it wounded me beyond words.

Others, of course, will not be in the least surprised when we tell them of our impending separation. On the basis of 'the onlooker sees most', many to whom we impart this news will have seen it coming for months, if not years. 'Oh!' they may say, 'You've finally seen the light'. In the middle of the struggle to save a failing marriage we will go to inordinate lengths to keep it on track, and in the process will often be deaf to what others are trying to tell us. We can receive a good deal of support and understanding from those from whom we least expected it. Some of our friends will welcome the news openly and these may represent the people who have made a similar decision themselves. No two separations are alike, however similar the circumstances may be; therefore cliché-comfort such as 'I know just how you feel' may be out of place. We just need permission to tell them how we feel, free from judgement and criticism. This releases us from much of the sense of failure we may otherwise experience.

On the basis of the distinction made earlier concerning our Being (who I am) and our Doing (what I do) it is vital that we make an appropriate response to our feelings of failure. Is it not more helpful to distinguish between failing as a person and failing in a project (like marriage)? Failure to pass an examination, for instance, does not make me a 'failure'. To fail to succeed in a project or a marriage is a failure to realize all that I hope for, and that brings its own sadness. But it is a serious mistake to identify ourselves in terms often quoted by people in distress after the break-up of a marriage: 'I'm a failure'. I recently read this sentence: 'I didn't fail in my marriage; I simply outgrew it.' Without wanting to diminish any appropriate responsibility for our part in the separation and the choices that we have made in ending a marriage, we do not have to carry the burden of guilt, shame and a sense of failure into the future. Very often it is found to be a matter of outgrowing a moribund relationship; and to discover that fact and act upon it in an adult way is far from representing failure. It is in fact success; something to be applauded and to take credit for. To cease to prolong the agony of an outworn marriage is a mark of maturity rather than failure. May it not be of significance that the Latin origin of 'fail' is *fallere*, 'to deceive'?

The following poem may be worth reading carefully. I value its healthy balance between taking all the blame for the ending of our marriage and taking no blame at all. It is instructive in presenting an appropriate balance of responsibility and a healthy model of how, even through the pain of a breakdown of a relationship, we can grow:

Reflections at the end of a marriage

We thought one got married and lived happily everafter;
  We didn't know that relationships require hard
    work . . .
We thought it wasn't any good if we had to ask for what
    we needed;
  We didn't know that no one is a mind reader . . .
We thought all our needs should have been filled with
    our marriage;
  We didn't know what our most important need was –
    a sense of self . . .
We thought our becoming one made us whole;
  We didn't know two whole people were necessary
    from the start . . .
We thought he had to be strong and take care of her;
  We didn't know we were supposed to take care of
    each other . . .
We thought it was disloyal to grow as an individual;
  We didn't know how stifling too much togetherness
    could be . . .
We thought that when the other grew, it was a threat;
  We didn't know we were good-enough, and shouldn't
    feel threatened . . .
We thought money would make us secure;
  We didn't know that security meant knowing you
    could make it, with or without money . . .
We thought those who went for help were weak;
  We didn't know that everyone needs help . . .
We thought the other wasn't giving;
  We didn't know we weren't taking in . . .
He thought I was happy;
  He didn't know how frightened I was . . .
I thought he was happy;

I didn't know how frightened he was . . .
We didn't know . . . We just didn't know . . .
There was so much we didn't know . . .

Susan Jeffers[18]

3. Three Case Studies

ANGELO: 'Tis one thing to be tempted, Escalus,
              Another thing to fall.
(William Shakespeare, *Measure for Measure*, II.i.17)

WHAT HAPPENS WHEN A RELATIONSHIP FAILS?

Every separation is, in part, unique to the two people concerned. Yet, without losing sight of the specifics of each couple, it is possible to discern common patterns in separation and leavetaking. In other words, although there may be an infinite variety of couples, there is no such infinite variety of causes of separation and divorce.

In this chapter I want to look at how some ordinary couples came to separate. The stories are given to provide background information to their relationship and to discover what led up to the crisis they eventually faced. I also want to tease out some of the issues which the people involved would need to face if they are to integrate their separation sufficiently to find future happiness, perhaps in another relationship. I am aware that by using only three couples I cannot hope to cover all the complexity of broken human relationships. However I hope to show that these couples' experiences can at least illustrate what are the important issues they may face.

Let us take as our first illustration the case of a couple who agreed mutually to end their marriage. I'll call them Molly and Ned.

The story of Molly and Ned

Molly and Ned have been married for ten years. They have two children. Ned says things went downhill after the second child went to school and Molly went back to full-time work. She held an important post in local government and felt fulfilled by her work. She was a popular member of staff and got on well with everyone. Her outdoor activities included tennis in summer and badminton in winter. Ned was more of a home bird; he enjoyed his occasional pint but preferred this in front of the telly where he would watch boxing and sport of any kind. They used to joke that whereas Molly did it, Ned only watched it. But there haven't been many jokes around recently.

Frankly, Molly began to experience Ned as a bit of a stick-in-the-mud. As a DIY fanatic he preferred to stay in and decorate or get involved in home improvements. He did not share her extrovert character and while in the early days of their marriage Molly could cope with this, she found it harder and harder to do so the longer the marriage went on.

Being a bit of a workaholic, Ned would often work overtime or bring work home with him. He began to see less of the children and correspondingly much of the burden for their care and entertainment fell upon Molly's shoulders. She resented this but never expressed it directly. Her feelings came out by investing less emotionally in the marriage, and by withdrawing sexually as much as she could. She enjoyed her friends at the sports club and began to see more of them. One night after the annual

Christmas party, Molly ended up in bed with Ted, one of the tennis coaches, and the fat was in the matrimonial fire when she arrived home the following morning. Ned questioned her on where she'd been and how frantic he felt and Molly agreed that she'd been rather unthinking not to have let Ned know where she was.

This episode was, in retrospect, a turning-point in their marriage. Molly wanted to see more of her lover and began to find ways to arrange this. Excitement was in her life again and she had not experienced that for ages. Eventually she told Ned what was happening and he was devastated. He moved into the spare bedroom immediately and a permafrost descended upon the relationship. Ned was no good at communicating at the best of times, and he now disappeared inside his shell. Truth to tell (only he wouldn't) he was deeply hurt. He felt angry and betrayed and furious with Molly for what she'd done – was doing – to him and the kids.

Things couldn't go on like that for ever, and one day Molly announced that she was leaving. She had decided to move in with Ted as soon as possible.

A number of issues then arose. The most important was what to do with the kids. Were they to go with Molly or stay with Ned? Ned was happy to keep them at home, where they had friends and where they could still go to the same school. He and Molly talked a bit about access and they finally agreed that they would come to tea with her on Wednesdays, and she would have them also each Saturday and for the whole of alternate weekends. The children were told about this and of course there were tears and fears expressed. Strangely, Molly and Ned seemed to cope with their feelings quite well and seemed to be acting as parents better than they had as husband and wife. Ned was on flexitime, so he could drop the kids off to school in the morning, and his mother, who lived nearby, would collect them in the afternoon and give them their tea at her house. Ned would collect them on his way home from work. Molly and he were both relieved that the best possible arrangements were being made for the ongoing care of their children.

For the time being they agreed that since Molly was working full-time, any maintenance wasn't necessary. Ned didn't know how he was going to cope financially anyway without Molly's income going into the family kitty. The mortgage would be the biggest problem, and Ned wondered if he should put the house up for sale and buy something smaller in the vicinity.

Molly began to sort out her things. She wanted to leave the house intact, but there were bits and pieces that had belonged to her mother that she would like to take with her. She sorted out her clothes and personal belongings and packed them in several suitcases. She did this while the children were out so as not to upset them. Molly also sorted out some of the family photograph albums to take with her. Ned arranged to take the children to the pictures while Ted and Molly came round to collect her stuff.

Realizing how difficult it would be when they got back, Ned arranged for a special tea and a video to watch afterwards. The children missed their mum at bedtime, and Ned arranged for them to speak to Molly on the telephone.

The next day Molly collected the children for the weekend. She took them back to Ted's house and introduced them to his two children. The four of them played for hours in the large garden and Ted seemed to take their presence in his stride. He had been widowed two years prior to his meeting Molly.

Ned and Molly continued to keep in contact especially about the finances and what to do with their small savings account and insurances. There was a lot to sort out, but they managed to do it in a spirit of amicability. Occasionally Ned would lose his temper with Molly and accuse her of being thoughtless and selfish, even though he knew in his heart that 'it takes two to tango' and he must have contributed in some way to the gradual deterioration of their relationship. Nine months later they were divorced.

Understanding Ned and Molly

This story looks briefly at how one couple managed their leavetaking process. It is not a general look at how couples manage such leavetaking, still less a blueprint of how it should be managed. It may help, however, as an illustration of how it *can* be done, for in truth we have only those models to go by that we have witnessed ourselves among our own family and friends.

Ned and Molly represent those couples whose eventual separation is a slow process. Analyzing that process we may discover the following issues:

1. Communication was allowed (by both Ned and Molly) to deteriorate. They simply stopped sharing their inner thoughts, dreams and needs. This is the most crucial area in which their relationship foundered.
2. There was little *honesty* between them concerning their dissatisfaction with the relationship.
3. Molly was *not confronting* Ned about the way she experienced him as a 'stick-in-the-mud'.
4. *Feelings* were not being expressed directly. Molly allowed her feelings to be suppressed and did not share them with Ned other than in indirect ways.
5. Ned allowed Molly's sexual withdrawal with-

out either *checking out* what it was about or expressing his feelings about her withdrawal.

6. There appear to have been no regular opportunities created for *prime time* sharing between them.

7. Ned and Molly stopped expressing *care and concern* for one another.

8. Neither of them noticed where most of their *energies* were being directed – Ned to his work, Molly to her sport.

9. There were dangerous levels of *assumption* in their relationship. Neither took the initiative to express what they really felt or needed.

10. Ned and Molly appear to have *passed responsibility* for their happiness to one another. Only when Molly took back responsibility for her own happiness did the crisis arise.

Each of these ten factors is like a 'knock-out' blow to a marriage. It is in fact possible for any one of them to cause the end of a relationship if left unattended, but the presence of more than two or three are usually found to be fatal to the marriage. As you ponder the break-up of some of your own previous relationships, perhaps you can now see from this map how they actually failed.

Thousands of Neds and Mollys eventually find themselves having to cope with the breakdown of their relationship. But not all of them end so amicably as that of Ned and Molly.

The story of Lisa and Martin

Lisa and Martin had a whirlwind holiday romance. They met on the plane going out to Spain, spent most of the holiday together, and Martin proposed on the return flight. It seemed that they had so much in common and their love was so real that it was, to them, a natural thing to plan for their marriage as soon as possible.

It was not long into the marriage that questions began to arise in Lisa's mind about Martin. He was very caring and attentive to her needs and their social life was as busy as ever; there was just this uneasy feeling that Martin was a bit of a closed book. On good days Lisa dismissed her uneasy feelings by attributing them to her sensitive nature. But on bad days she began to question whether her mother was right: 'Marry in haste, repent at leisure'.

Martin began to be inexplicably absent from time to time. His excuses always seemed to be plausible, but cumulatively they left big gaps. The crunch came one morning when Lisa returned home unexpectedly and found Martin in bed with his friend George.

All Lisa's feelings of unease and suspicion were fully vindicated. But nothing she had felt before had prepared her for this shock. It was truly a bolt from the blue and in her state of utter trauma and humiliation she ran out of the house and went round to her mother's. She stayed there for a few days trying to sort out her feelings before she could bring herself to speak to Martin again. He had been ringing Lisa but her mother told him she was not ready to speak to him.

Eventually they arranged to meet on neutral ground at a local pub. Martin was very tense, and Lisa was by this time still withdrawn and not really wanting to say anything to Martin at all. She sat and listened to what Martin had to say with increasing amazement. He had been to see a counsellor as soon as Lisa had left, a decision he had been putting off for the past ten years ever since his first homosexual fantasies arose. He had finally to admit that he was bisexual and felt attracted to both sexes on an almost equal basis. He had always hoped that his marriage would be the 'glue' that would keep him orientated within his heterosexual urges, but this proved not to be strong enough. His attraction to George and his discovery that George was 'gay' eventually led to their going to bed together.

Lisa was furious. She felt a blazing anger which came out in all directions. She was angry with Martin for his duplicity and for not sharing that part of himself with her (so that was why she was experiencing Martin as a bit of a closed book!); and with George's knowing Martin was married; and angry for allowing herself to be duped by Martin. Under the surface, and not yet fully conscious, were her feelings of humiliation and betrayal. She would later feel that Martin had used her as an insurance against his homosexual part emerging in the future.

The marriage ended then and there. Lisa was sure she wanted a divorce as soon as practical. She wanted Martin to sell the house so that she could buy another property; living with mother was no final solution. By arrangement Lisa came round with her father to collect the personal belongings she needed, and later when their house was sold she agreed to a split of the furniture. The divorce went through quickly on the basis of Martin's unreasonable behaviour and was uncontested. Lisa never wanted to see Martin again.

Understanding Martin and Lisa

What are some of the issues in the story of Martin and Lisa that they would eventually need to address?

Martin	Lisa
1. His sexual orientation and his choices for future sexual expression.	1. Her feelings of humiliation, anger and possible disgust.

2. Guilt at having hurt Lisa.

3. Grief at letting Lisa go, whom he still loved.

4. Shame and doubt regarding his relationship with George.

5. Reaction to the divorce by family and friends.

6. His standing in the wider community and at work.

7. Anger with Lisa for her rejection and lack of understanding.

8. His future contacts with women.

9. Responsibility for 'safe sex'.

10. Changes in his personal identity and view of himself.

2. Ambivalence in her feelings towards Martin: love/hate.

3. Grief at the ending of her marriage.

4. Doubts regarding her own sexuality; had she failed Martin in this area?

5. Feeling stupid at her lack of awareness and her disregard of her intuition.

6. Guilt. Had she been too severe in her reactions to Martin?

7. Loss of trust in men and how this would affect her future happiness.

8. Loss of her personal self-esteem.

9. The healing of her deep inner pain and hurt.

10. Her return to singleness including living alone for the first time.

Again we can see how each individual separation raises enormous issues for each of the partners. What they do with these issues is, of course, up to them. For most couples parting, I would say it is true that they will be largely unaware of such a huge agenda. In the immediate concern for survival and the practical matters of the divorce (are couples that have never faced legal separation and divorce aware of the amount of paperwork that such an act demands?) their inner feelings and deeper psychological needs may well be either denied or overlooked. To the extent that this is so, such unresolved issues may contaminate not only their leavetaking process but any subsequent relationship which they may pursue.

Both in the case of Ned and Molly and that of Lisa and Martin there were at least fairly clean breaks. The issues became clear: Molly's affair with Ted and Martin's affair with George both brought about a crisis in their existing relationship. Whatever may have been the predisposing causes to these crises, the end of their marriages was swift and sudden. So let us look at another story in which the ending is not so sudden and the leavetaking not so swift and clear-cut.

The story of Eric and Joy

Eric and Joy were teenage lovers from their schooldays. Joy became pregnant at sixteen and left school early to have the baby. Joint parental pressure produced an ill-advised marriage when the baby was a few months old. In the early days their love and optimism seemed enough to get them through the problems they had to face: setting up a home together and providing for little Joey. They were determined to show the world that they could manage. They were both survivors.

Psychologically, it meant a very large gap in their personal development. Hardly had their childhood ended than they became parents. They had virtually no older teenage years other than as parents to little Joey. They had no experience of singleness or of living alone. Neither had they the experience of a wider range of loving and intimate relationships before choosing their life partner. For Joy in particular it meant that her education was curtailed and she left school without taking any GCSE examinations. This also dashed her hopes for a satisfying job in the future. Eric went on to further education at the local polytechnic in pursuit of a BSc degree in engineering.

Living on Eric's grant and some social security payments was no picnic, but they managed. The strain began to tell on Joy in Eric's final year as his energies went more on his studies, and less on Joy and Joey. He began to get impatient with Joey and found his natural noises and boisterousness interfering with his work. He spent more time out of the house than inside it, and was tired out when he did eventually come home. All this work created in Eric the need for time to play, and since babysitters were hard to come by it transpired that Eric was out most of the time. Joy began to feel disheartened and angry. On the one hand she knew that Eric was working for their future and felt guilty about wanting him to spend more time with her and Joey; but on the other hand she felt that he should be more understanding of her needs and those of their baby.

Joy turned to her mother for help. She found herself spending more time at mother's and the other siblings having flown the nest, Joy's mother rather enjoyed having her daughter and grandson around the house. It was at this point that the pressures within the marriage began to become both visible and vocal.

Eric complained of the time Joy was spending at her mother's. His meals were not ready; the house seemed like a tip. The washing and ironing were not done and he was under pressure at the polytechnic as his finals approached. Joy now complained at the time Eric spent on his studies and at the poly. She wondered if this was

all there was to it, indicating her suspicions that Eric
may be seeing someone else. A full-scale row ensued and
eventually Eric swept out of the house and went back to
his mother's place.

It may have been a familiar marital squabble that would
have healed once a few hours had intervened, but this did
not happen. Eric did not return the following day, and
when Joy rang his mother she was decidedly 'off' and had
no idea when Eric would return. In fact Eric wanted some
time to think and to study without hassle. His mother,
like Joy's rather liked having her boy back home to fuss
over. Eric was twenty-one and Joy now seventeen, and
Eric's mother had never been in favour of their marrying
so young. What might have been a few hours apart grew
into a week.

Joy wrote to Eric wanting to know where she stood
with him and when he would return. Eric had in the
intervening time thrown himself into his studies and rather
enjoyed not having to get home as soon as lectures ended.
He found the social life at the poly as novel as it was
refreshing. He began to resent the teenage years he had
lost through marrying Joy, and his temporary return to
singleness eventually led to a permanent state of separation.

Joy was devastated. It seemed to her that the row was
a convenient excuse for Eric to dump her and Joey and
go off and enjoy himself, leaving her to pick up the pieces.
She gave up the council house, and returned to live with
her mother. The release from responsibility as a husband
and a father came to Eric as a welcome relief, and to be
pampered by his mother again was just too convenient to
lose.

To the rest of the two families it was just as they had
predicted. Variations on the theme of 'I told them so'
were often heard and no one seemed a bit surprised when

the marriage came to an end. But although the marriage was over it was far from finished as far as Joy was concerned. Her feelings of betrayal and anger spilled over into a very spiteful campaign of intimidation and revenge.

None of the times that Eric wanted to see Joey were 'convenient' for Joy. She would make sure she was out on some errand or other. She wrote to Eric demanding money, although she had already emptied the small bank account containing the remainder of his grant money. Joy would push Joey round to Eric's mother's house and create scenes on the doorstep, much to the embarrassment of her mother-in-law and the neighbours. On one occasion Eric had defended himself against Joy's physical assault, causing a bruise on her face, but she then called the police and demanded protection. Just before Eric's finals, Joy came round in a rage. Her suppressed feelings of resentment about the termination of her education due to the pregnancy finally surfaced and she was determined to make Eric pay for that. She threatened him with a knife and Eric's mother finally called the police to have her taken away. Joy's mother then got involved, accusing Eric's mother of putting her daughter in prison and a full-scale feud was in the making. Eric's concentration was disturbed and he felt in no condition to take his first paper the following morning. He felt that Joy had deliberately sabotaged his chances of success.

Joy fought Eric every inch of the way concerning the custody of the baby Joey. She made out that he was unfit as a father and her affidavit to her solicitor made it sound like a character assassination. Eventually care and control went to Joy and she continued to make it as difficult as possible for Eric to see Joey. Finally he gave up trying. They were divorced five months later. Before that time was up, however, Joy was being seen with another man who had been divorced a few years ago and who had two children of his own. Eric got his degree, albeit third class honours, and soon moved away to his first real job.

Understanding Eric and Joy

One of the more positive aspects of this separation is that they were young enough to pick up the pieces and make a new life for themselves. They both admitted in the end that the marriage had been a mistake, and their defiance and determination to show that they could manage on their own was finally seen to be unfounded. It was more a challenge to their ability to cope than the love affair of the century! Joey, of course, was the permanent loser. He lost his natural father and it would be many years before he could learn who he was and decide whether or not to make contact.

The story of Eric and Joy is one of allowing small issues to grow into big and, eventually, unmanagable ones. They do not seem to have given time and effort into becoming a couple; they were essentially still single in their attitudes towards life and to one another. They were, in effect, 'playing house'. It may be called the Hansel and Gretel marriage, two babes in the wood playing at grown-ups. Being catapulted into parenthood before their own growing up period had ended placed enormous burdens upon both of them. There was so much of their life that had not been lived before they chose to 'settle down'. There were deep and hidden scripts of an unfulfilled adolescence that simply would not go away. They were not sufficiently adult in their attitudes to commitment to sustain the kind of pressures that parenthood, comparative poverty and full-time study would place upon their relationship. Joy's childish reactions were merely the acting out of her emotional age. So much had been expected of her and she was, at first, determined to cope; but the emotional resources and wisdom simply were not there and she did not know how to react to Eric once she felt the pull and the attraction of being cared for by her mother. Psychologically, she still needed mother's care and to lose responsibility for Joey occasionally. Eric, too, had not been prepared for leaving home and he had not appreciated fully what a total commitment to a marriage would mean or cost him. At twenty-one he found himself a graduate, an engineer and divorced. He had to work hard at putting Joey out of his mind but he was not always successful. His grief often got the better of him, but letters to Joy enquiring about Joey were returned unopened. Joey's photograph was his only consolation, as he contemplated losing out on all the important days of Joey's childhood.

These three stories attempt to outline some of the issues involved in leavetaking. Taken at random they illustrate the enormous divergences both in the reasons for couples parting and in the ways in which separation is conducted. So much depends on the characters of the couple concerned, their maturity (or lack of it), their ability to cope in a crisis, their self-understanding and their ability to express their feelings. Thousands of marriages are conducted on the principle of 'Well, let's just hope for the best' or even 'Let's hope the worst does not happen!' Life teaches us that such simplistic notions are totally unrealistic and form no useful defence against the worst happening. Of course, not every disaster is either foreseen or provided for in our calculations. The occasional storm and tempest can rock the safest of marital boats; on such occasions it is not the strength of the wind that matters so much as the strength of the anchor!

Too many marriages rely on problems simply not arising, rather than spending time and energy on securing the foundations of the relationship. Unless these are well-founded they are simply accidents looking for somewhere to happen. It is in the day-to-day communications, sharing, caring and openness that such foundations are laid, not as a panic measure against failure but because relationships that are not busy growing are busy dying.

These three couples alert us not only to the ease with which some relationships can come apart but also to the important issues that are left over once the relationship ends. It will be in direct proportion to how those issues are dealt with successfully after the leavetaking that their future happiness depends. Is there a creative way ahead for such leavetaking?

4. The Common Ground in Marital Break-up

Why people divorce each other is their own business, inscrutable. They seldom, in my experience, know why themselves – know what was more important, I mean, along the camps of the Everest of dissatisfactions nearly any human being feels with any other human being he knows inside out. Maybe nothing is most important. It's the mountain, and you must get too weary to climb on.

(John Berryman, *The Freedom of the Poet*, 1976)

In common with other emergency features, like fire escapes and smoke alarms, divorce has become part of our way of life.

To the outsiders, especially the unmarried or the happily married, divorce figures may be shocking. Frankly criticism or 'tut-tutting' by those not involved is not constructive in the great divorce debate. But figures alone don't tell the whole story.

To the insiders, actually involved in the process of separation, things look very different. At the moment of the break-up of their marriage, theirs is the only relationship that matters. Like most experiences of pain, ours is always worse than anyone else's.

For a conservative estimate of couples separating – which includes those living as married as well as divorce statistics – we are clearly looking at about 200,000 partnerships that break up every year. Is there anything, apart from the act of separation, that approximately 400,000 people could have in common? To be sure, each union is unique to the two people whose 'marital fingerprints' make it their very own, and no two couples are exactly alike. Does this mean, therefore, that we cannot find any common ground in marital separation?

First we must rid our minds of the idea that every break-up is an unmitigated tragedy. It is easy to think of separation along these lines – and, of course, this *is* sometimes the case – but we need to check out the assumption.

Separation and divorce are not always – and certainly not necessarily – bad things. Thousands of people have found new life and happiness after separation from a dead or moribund marriage. Some marriages should not have happened in the first place and, when this is discovered, a mature response is not to prolong the agony but to find an amicable way of ending it. The anti-divorce lobby does not accept this point but sees marriage as made in heaven and existing 'till death us do part'; a concept which in modern practice is honoured more in the breach than in the observance. It mistakes the intention for the reality. Promises of lifelong partnership are an ideal, towards which many people entertain mental reservations. They would prefer not to promise the impossible. It may not be widely appreciated that when these words were written into the wedding service, life expectancy was not much above thirty-five years. Today we are in a totally different socio-economic situation where the long-distance marriage is welded to increasing longevity. In the United States of America, there is a common practice of signing pre-nuptial agreements, by which claims on one another are set out against the time when (not if) the marriage fails. At least there is some realism in such arrangements. The British Law Commission is, in fact, considering putting forward similar proposals.

At this point, for the purposes of simplification, I want to suggest a chronological map, since the *time-factor* is a common denominator in all separations. I will put forward a scheme of four phases as a way of making sense of the separation process which all separating couples will have to negotiate. Of course, the actual time spent in each of these four chronological phases will vary enormously (like any other period of grief and bereavement) and will be related to the length and depth of the relationship which is ending. For those of you on the brink of separation, I hope to provide a guide to the kind of things you may expect as you face the implications of your decision – or that of your spouse. I believe this map of the separation process speaks similarly to both parties to the marriage.

THE FOUR PHASES OF MARITAL BREAK-UP

In our suggested Marital Break-Up Map, what may we identify as the four phases that we can expect to have to go through?

I   The preparation phase: process = breaking down

This covers the period of the breaking down of the relationship and the act of separating:

> Key experiences: Shock
> Grief
> Disorientation
> Fear
> Family reactions

II   The intermediate phase: process = breaking out

This period covers how we cope with the separation, change and loss, and immediate survival plans:

Key experiences: Anxiety
                   Isolation
                   Pain
                   Depression
                   Guilt
                   Anger

III   The consolidation phase: process = breaking in

In this period we learn how to cope with singleness, and how to let go of the old relationship:

Key experiences: Growing confidence
                   Getting used to a new reality
                   Fresh bouts of grief or anger

IV   The future phase: process = breaking through

This is an open-ended experience in which new hopes and dreams as well as healing from the pain of the past are the dominant themes:

Key experiences: Hope
                   The need to share
                   Ability to risk new relationships
                   The need to be loved
                   A new partner?

Each of these phases will need further explanation.

5. The Four Phases of Marital Break-up

I THE PREPARATION PHASE

TORVALD: But to leave your home – your husband and your children . . . You haven't thought of what people will say.

NORAH: I can't consider that. All I know is that this is necessary for me.

(Henrik Ibsen, *A Doll's House*, 1879)

In this phase I include the run-up to the separation which in practice can vary from years to moments, and from a carefully planned withdrawal to a sudden and unexpected departure. There is an enormous variation in what a preparation period can mean; indeed some people might deny there was any such thing. 'I came home one day, and she'd gone!' In that case, he felt totally unprepared. Nevertheless it is almost always true that, on further reflection or enquiry, something has being going on in the relationship (known or unknown) to bring one of the partners to that point of sudden departure. Using the similarity of some illnesses, there is usually a period of 'incubation' when the bugs have got in but have not yet shown themselves in a fully-blown, diagnosable illness. Marriages, too, can show signs that they are sickening for something! What might some of these be?

Warning signs that a partnership is in trouble

Maureen Lipman (my number one funny-girl) tells the story of one of her appearances on a women's chat show. The chairperson asked her seriously, 'What do you think is the sign that a marriage is in trouble?' Maureen thought for a moment and then replied outrageously, 'A marriage is in serious trouble when he masturbates in bed and then turns to his wife and asks, "How was it for you?" '

Behind the comedy is an element of truth. Private masturbation is a well-known escape hatch in a faltering relationship. Escape hatches are traditionally those exits that we use to get our needs met when the relationship is not going well. Marital therapist Harville Hendrix has accrued over 300 answers to his question, 'What does your spouse do to avoid you?' Here are just a few:

- read romantic novels
- disappearing into the garage
- camping out on the phone
- worshipping the car
- spending too much time with the kids
- volunteering for every committee at church
- avoiding eye contact
- falling asleep on the couch
- coming home late for dinner
- being sick and tired all the time
- not wanting to be touched
- lying
- jogging ten miles a day
- going shopping

- keeping separate bank accounts
- masturbating[19]

These are some of the observable (but not always observed) 'marital bugs' that are already within the system – perhaps each of them either entirely neutral or even at times desirable. 'After all,' we may argue, 'we must go shopping sometimes. And,' we may add, 'don't we need to be separate some of the time? It's unhealthy to live in each other's pocket!' Yes, that's true; yet there is all the difference between breathing spaces (vital to the well-being of the individual) and escape hatches. Breathing spaces help to revive our flagging autonomy and separateness and the need to pursue our own interests and hobbies; escape hatches are (often unconscious) ways of avoiding full interaction with our partner. It is precisely at this point that we meet one of the continuing stresses in a marriage: *how can I be fully committed to this relationship while at the same time developing as a separate, autonomous individual?* There is a precarious balancing act being performed between these two issues in every marriage, and the fact that we are ignorant of this only makes the potential harm all the worse.[20]

As you contemplate your own impending or actual separation, do you not now recognize – and can actually name – the marital bugs that helped towards the demise of your marriage? You may even be kicking yourself for having failed to spot these warning signs.

But not all marital bugs are easy to identify.

Hidden factors

Although the departure of a partner may be described as a 'sudden shock', some factors have been operating invisibly over a period of time. As Christopher Clulow and Janet

Mattinson write: 'The departure of love is seldom an abrupt event in marriage. It is, rather, a gradual erosion which occurs over years as a result of neglect.'[21]

My daughter Jill rang one day to tell me that the roof of her utility room had suddenly collapsed. It had seemed all right in the morning; by night it had caved in. On further enquiry, however, the builders found that the roof had been unsafe for years due to the penetration of wet-rot. One day, almost by chance, it could take no more strain and collapsed. This seems to me to be a useful illustration of what can happen in some marriages. Like the roof, the marriage has been there for years, and there have been no warning signs until the relationship suddenly and irretrievably breaks down. (An interesting after-thought occurs to me. My wife, who is asthmatic, often used to come out of that utility room with breathing difficulties! She was convinced that there was deep pene-tration of water producing the fungus, against which she reacted quite violently. She, at least, was not a bit sur-prised to hear about the roof!)

Some relationships experience a sudden and unexpected collapse, while others take place over a longer period. It is here that generalizations are hard to make and perhaps could be dangerous.

Can these 'preparation periods' be accurately assessed in any case? Some couples are very clear when the 'rot' set in. They recall the unexplained absences, the telephone calls that hang up without speaking, the summer confer-ence with the Open University, the lack of interest, and suddenly they all 'make sense'. In an informative article Phillip Hodson writes:

> The process begins with elimination. In order for an affair to happen, a spouse-errant must devote time, sexuality, organization, money and subterfuge to the

event . . . Even abbreviated, truncated, interrupted, coition is time-consuming. Laugh if he says he's about to take up poker: Freud is listening. It's too pat to offer such an easy excuse for playing games in the small hours. Uncharacteristic sociability? Unprecedented devotion to work? Four punctures a month? One woman I know took up the flute and tooted her way throughout north London for five years before her husband requested a recital. She still couldn't manage one musical note.[22]

Affairs, however, are but one way in which the marital rot sets in. Nature abhors a vacuum, and where there are long-term needs being ignored or neglected the structure of the marriage is already at risk. Growing apart gradually, and almost imperceptibly, is the way some marriages are undermined. From doing everything together, they gradually do nothing together. They live separate lives.

I recall one clergyman who was invited to consider the offer of a large inner-city church as his next pastoral charge. The churchwardens showed him the parish and the church, and finally they came to the vicarage. The minister noticed that the vicarage was divided in half. There were two of everything, and he enquired if the previous vicar had lodgers. Rather shame-facedly the wardens confessed that the vicar and his wife did not get on, and that they had lived separate lives within the vicarage for the past ten years. They managed to keep up the front of a stable marriage, but once inside the vicarage they never spoke to each other.

The LAT syndrome

Rabbi Lionel Blue refers to this as the LAT syndrome, Living Apart Together. Since, in the case of the vicar and his wife, a separation might have scandalized the parish, they had chosen the way of deception in order to keep up appearances. Many marriages considered stable and sound are of the LAT variety. Simple economics may dictate this uneasy status quo. It is not everyone who can easily walk away from a dead marriage.

Some couples with the LAT syndrome manage to maintain an amicability while going their separate ways. The advantages of this pattern include staying together for the children; not having to split up the family; giving both partners maximum security; freedom from the marriage contract in honesty and integrity; and the freedom to develop other relationships while respecting the feelings of the other partner by not bringing extra-marital lovers into the matrimonial home. Of course in practice there is a wide variety of choices within the LAT syndrome, but it does afford some people at least a breathing space while other, perhaps more permanent, arrangements can be made for their separate futures. An agreement to separate can just as easily be thwarted nowadays by the difficulties in selling the matrimonial home. This necessitates couples living together in a state of apprehension and sometimes acrimonious disharmony for many months, sometimes for years. Fear, of course, is another reason why people don't separate as Shirley Valentine admitted:

> 'An' I know what you're saying'. You're sayin' what Jane always says – why don't I leave? An' the fact of the matter is – I don't know why. I don't know why anyone should put up with a situation in which a forty-two-year-old woman has the opportunity of fulfillin' a dream, of travellin', just a little bit, just two weeks of the year, an' can't do it. I don't know why . . . I just know that if y' described me to me, I'd say you were tellin' me a joke. I don't know why

I stay. I hate it. I hate the joke of it . . . I'm terrified if y' want to know. I'm terrified that if I left him, I'd have nowhere to go, an' I'd find that there was no place for me in the life beyond the wall . . . So I stay.'[23]

There is always, of course, the possibility of the sudden and unexpected disappearance of a spouse (perhaps the children too) to contend with. It is usually known as the 'Dear John' syndrome.

The 'Dear John' syndrome

This describes the scenario when a husband arrives home from work to find his wife and family gone, and a letter on the mantelpiece informing him that they are not coming back. One husband I spoke to, who had been going through a sticky patch in his marriage, arrived home at lunchtime to find his wife and child – and most of the furniture – gone. The 'Dear John' letter merely gave the name and address of a solicitor through whom he could make further contact. He was distraught.

To be sure, there is also a 'Dear Jane' syndrome. Women do not have an exclusive right on sudden disappearance. On many occasions it is the husband who unexpectedly vanishes.

In terms of the leavetaking process, this is often known as the 'bridge-cutting' style of ending a relationship. It is swift, sharp and unannounced. It is the equivalent of a sudden and unexpected death in the family. Similar emotions are released: shock, numbness, unbelief and a sense of disorientation and unreality.

Later other emotions arise: a feeling of abandonment and rejection, and a rising sense of anger and betrayal. More, we often feel a fool for having turned a blind eye to recent events and for hoping for the best, and begin to blame ourselves with relentless vigour. An appropriate feeling of outrage can often be turned inwards against ourselves and become an 'inrage'.

The person leaving may have a slightly different set of feelings. The most immediate is sometimes an enormous sense of relief at having made the break. Somewhere they have found the strength and courage to admit that, from their standpoint at least, the relationship was over. Feelings of shame and guilt may or may not follow, depending on their personality and the degree of insight into their own inner world. It is often the case that a vanishing partner is wracked by guilt and anxiety about how the family is coping in their absence. Others, of course, never give a second thought to what has been left behind. Where a spouse goes to live with someone else – a familiar reason for leaving the matrimonial home – this can give rise to a complicated pattern of behaviour that I call the Yo-Yo syndrome.

The Yo-Yo syndrome

This describes what happens when a person leaves a spouse to live with someone else, only to experience colossal feelings of guilt for having hurt their wife or husband. One solution is to run back home. These feelings of guilt may or may not be compounded by the calls of a helpless, abandoned spouse trying to cope with a distraught family. Finally overcome with guilt and remorse, the spouse returns to the family home. But then he/she is overcome with guilt concerning the 'third party' whom they have now abandoned. Telephone calls, further meetings, and in no time at all, he/she has left home again and settled back with the other person. This process can go on indefinitely. Like a yo-yo, they are for ever going up and down between two people, neither of whom they want to hurt. They find it impossible to cope with the fact that, whoever they eventually choose, someone is going to feel desperately hurt.

But we can't have everything in life, and we certainly cannot please all the people all the time. Having got into the 'eternal triangle', at least two of the people involved are going to experience hurt and pain. This is where another factor enters to complicate the picture. Having made the break from a dead or dying marriage, that person brings their hurt and pain into the new relationship. It is another facet of the leavetaking process which I will describe as the Prometheus factor.

The Prometheus factor

In the Greek myths Prometheus (meaning Forethought) had helped to create Man. Wishing to bestow upon Man some great power, Prometheus decided that fire alone could be the gift. But at this point a difficulty arose. Fire was the special possession and prerogative of the gods, and Prometheus knew they would never part with this gift. Prometheus set out for Mount Olympus and, entering unobserved, stole a fire-brand and conveyed the gift of fire to Man. Eventually Jupiter observed the fire on earth and exacted terrible punishment upon Prometheus. He was bound to a rock and:

> a voracious vulture was summoned to feast day by day upon his liver, the tearing of which from his side by the bird's cruel beak and talons caused the sufferer intense anguish. All day long the vulture gorged himself; but during the cool night, while the bird slept, Prometheus' suffering abated, and the liver grew again, thus prolonging the torture, which bade fair to have no end.[24]

Prometheus had undoubtedly stolen a tremendous gift, but at such a terrible cost. No metaphor can be applied bluntly to every case of marital separation and I am focusing upon only one facet, but it is an important one. Many people gain their separation at a high cost, and usually it is the subsequent relationship that ends up paying the bill. I think of those whose former spouses will not let them go, and let things be. The cost to the third party is often unbearable. One ex-wife, twelve years after her divorce, is still pursuing her ex-husband in a manner resembling the voracious vulture that plagued Prometheus daily. The vicious games are unrelenting. At the weddings of their children, this wife demands precedence of place, refuses to attend if her ex-husband's wife attends and literally blackmails her children into submission to her demands. She placed the ex-husband's Christmas presents for the children in the dustbin, informing her children that he had obviously forgotten them and wanted no further contact with them.

The Prometheus factor shows us the high price that can be exacted for separation. The husband's new wife has borne a heavy cost at the hands of an unforgiving, and unrelenting ex-wife. On many occasions it is the second wife who ends up having to work in order to pay the maintenance to her husband's former wife. Of course, men also can exact revenge upon their former wives, sometimes resorting to physical violence or threats against the new man in her life. Maintenance payments can bleed some men white, placing an even greater strain on any new relationship. Those of you who have seen the horrendous American film, *Fatal Attraction*, will know the kind of viciousness that can ensue when a person is jilted. In the film, Dan Gallagher meets Alex and they spend a steamy weekend together. However, Alex is a very disturbed woman, showing hysterical and pathological reactions to the end of the affair. Her vengeance wreaked upon Dan and his family is horrifying. Here is another version of the Prometheus factor, this time by an ex-lover and not the wife. In both cases there is a crippling cost exacted on the so-called 'guilty' party. Some second or subsequent marriages are strained beyond measure by such behaviour and it is difficult to avoid the conclusion that this is precisely what the abandoned partner/lover intends to happen. 'I'll show him!' or 'I'll make her wish she'd never been born!' bear all the hallmarks of revenge elevated to an art form. 'Hell hath no fury . . .' is by no means limited to the female of the species! George Bernard Shaw's famous dictum comes true: 'What God hath joined together no man ever shall put asunder: God will take care of that.'[25]

Affairs, while usually getting wide interest and narrow criticism, are not the only signs of the beginning of the end of a relationship. There are the almost imperceptible factors, none of which individually may seem of any special interest, but over a period erode the content of meaningfulness from a relationship. Marcus spoke of the people he met on a training course who found him witty and attractive, while at home he was constantly criticized and denigrated by his wife. It is easy, of course, to play the wit and the clown when he is away from home and the family and in fact to act a part in order to gain interest and approval. Yet the contrast was so great in the way he was treated that it led him to make a total reappraisal of his own self-esteem. He found there were many negative features which he had simply taken on board, unthinkingly, from his wife and when he decided to confront her about them it was the beginning of the end of the marriage. Personal growth can be by far the biggest factor in the breaking down of a relationship. It is the point at which the worm turns.

Key experiences

I have already strayed into the important realm of human feelings, and it may be useful at this point to focus upon the great variety of feelings present when a marriage ends. This reminds us how difficult it is to describe just one facet of a separation when the whole of a human being is engaged in the process.

Whatever the circumstances surrounding the separation, and regardless of whether it is sudden or planned, there are going to be emotions experienced by both parties. These may range from ecstatic joy to suicidal misery. As the variations are so infinite it is not easy to predict which will be uppermost in any particular couple's separation. Some feelings may be included in the following themes and variations:

Theme	Variations
shock	agitation, unbelief, denial, desperation
grief	sadness, sense of loss, feelings of abandonment, isolation, helplessness
disorientation	knocked off balance, not knowing what to do next, frantic need for security
fear	anxiety and rising panic, awareness of lack of inner resources
family reaction	telling the family, experiencing blame or responsibility for the breakdown, accepting understanding and sympathy

Such feelings and their varying shades of experience do not come all at once. Often they come in waves, first one then the others. We move in and out of these feelings according to mood or the circumstances of the moment. Like any experience of bereavement, our feelings of loss will be expressed in different ways. A death, for instance, we sometimes may describe as a 'blessed release', and many people say this of the death of their marriage.

While these and others will be the immediate experience of the partner who has been left, different feelings may be experienced by the partner who leaves. There could be great elation that finally they have burst the matrimonial boil and have successfully negotiated their exit from it. They are often amazed at their own inner strength in getting out of a hopeless arrangement where both parties were hurting one another continually. They may experience disorientation as they adjust to a new environment, and (since the partner who leaves usually gets most of the blame for the situation) will doubtless come in for much criticism in leaving the marriage. This will depend largely on the religious or moral convictions of the one expressing their opinion. Yet, more and more, we are coming to understand as a society that the partner who leaves is not necessarily the 'guilty party'. Indeed they could be described as the more honest in facing facts.

If this is the period of breaking down, what is the next phase that we need to negotiate?

6. The Four Phases of Marital Break-up

II THE INTERMEDIATE PHASE

Each ex-partner must first acknowledge the loss and mourn the dreams and hopes that were never fully realized and never will be realized. It is important to cry, for only crying reduces anger to human size. And only by mourning can a person regain or maintain perspective on what was lost. And only by mourning will the adults be able to close the door and move on. Even the most miserable marriage embodied some expectation of a better life, companionship, love and esteem, and although no tears may be shed for the lost partner, the symbolic meaning of the marriage should be put to rest with gentleness.

(Judith S. Wallerstein and Sandra Blakeslee)[26]

This part of our leavetaking map tries to take account of what happens after the initial separation has occurred and we have experienced some (or all) of the emotions outlined in Chapter 5. In chronological terms, this phase can take anything from a few days to a year or more. Since some of us are constitutionally better equipped than others to cope with loss, there will be very wide variations.

What I have in mind is to outline the broad question, 'What do I do now?' after we have separated from our partner. After the breaking down of the relationship we need to come to terms with the 'breaking out' of the old patterns associated with that previous relationship. Since such patterns of intimacy and togetherness may have been built up over many years (my first marriage lasted over twenty-five years) there is no way in which they are going to disappear suddenly. This is precisely the problem we face when a partner dies: how do we 'uncouple' and become single again? Separation is a kind of death, but in what specific way does the metaphor fit?

We cannot begin to answer this question without looking at the wider social attitudes in our culture towards death and dying. In particular we need to address the widespread avoidance of the subject of death and, by implication, any healthy models in coming to terms with it.

The denial of death

'It was a marriage doomed to flicker and die,' said Nick Constable, writing in *Today*,[27] concerning the ending of the marriage between Elton John and Renate Blauel. It was said that Elton's flamboyant lifestyle, combined with his self-confessed bisexual orientation and history of depression and suicide attempts, made the union untenable.

Are some marriages doomed to 'flicker and die'? And what happens when they do? These important questions have a relevance far wider than the context of marriage. I see them as part of an ongoing social and philosophical discussion, concerning what Ernest Becker, in his Pulitzer prize-winning book, called *The Denial of Death*. In a meta-phorical way, relationships can also 'die'; that is, they lose their meaning and purpose, the love between two people evaporates, friends become enemies and love turns to hate. These are the facts. But we have an uncanny way of denying such unpalatable truths. We are always busy denying and avoiding death, no matter what form it takes. In our map of marital leavetaking it is frequently found to be a major factor in this intermediate phase and there is no doubt that, by such hanging-on devices, we prolong much of our agony.

We must not expect it to be otherwise when considering the ending of an important relationship. That, too, involves a kind of 'death' experience in terms of its finality and its unwelcome nature. In my opinion, it is not death that is at fault, but our inadequate and often immature reactions to it. We have all become experts at avoiding the painfully obvious merely because in admitting it we shall have to deal with it. Having owned it, we must take responsibility for it. Rather than do this, we choose to go on denying it.

Nothing reveals our cultural inadequacies more than our attitudes towards death. In many places, death is the biggest of all cultural taboos. Such denial can ascend to ludicrous heights. An elderly couple were walking along a street in Nottingham. They stopped for a rest and a chat. 'You know, my dear,' the husband said to his wife gently, 'when one of us dies, I shall go to live in Bourne-mouth.' The truth is that we lack adequate models for dealing with death in its many forms: physical death, separation and divorce, redundancies and unemployment, the children leaving home, the loss of role, prestige and power through retirement, and ultimately perhaps the loss of our precious independence. These are just a few of the many losses we can expect to experience in our lives, and some of us are ill-prepared to meet them through our processes of avoidance and denial.

Others, of course, are so convinced that their relationships are doomed to end in failure that they spend an enormous amount of energy insuring against such losses. It may be compared to taking out an insurance policy against its failure, not recognizing that the premiums actually rob the marriage of necessary life and resources and (above all) commitment. In fact they bring about the death they actually fear! What may some of the devices we can identify in taking out an insurance on your marriage look like?

Death-dealing models

'Drop before you're dropped!'

When some people go into marriage 'knowing' it is bound to fail (the reasons do not matter here), they do not give 100 per cent commitment to the relationship. So they hold back their physical, emotional and sexual commitment to the marriage. They resemble the client referred to as Rachel in M. Scott Peck's illuminating book, *The Road Less Travelled*. Rachel had a disastrous history of broken relationships with men and entered therapy to get to the root of her problems. She seemed to live in a world populated with rejecting males whom she appeared to attract with unerring regularity. The problem turned out to be that Rachel had had no firm commitment to her by her parents and that her earliest experiences were of rejection. She took these feelings, still gift-wrapped, into every relationship she had and of course the inevitable always happened.

Rachel was tied up with the 'I'll desert you before you desert me' syndrome. There are many people whose motto is 'Drop before you're dropped!' *By withholding commitment in her relationships, she was in fact setting up their demise.* That was her insurance policy against pain. As Scott Peck writes: 'For Rachel, "letting go", sexually or otherwise, represented a commitment of herself, and she was unwilling to make a commitment when the map of her past experience made it seem certain she would not receive any commitment in return.'[28] Rachel's parting shot to her husband was, 'I'm not going to give myself to you when I know damn well that you're going to dump me one of these days!'[29]

The Rachels (or Raymonds) of this world enter into marriage from behind their defensive barriers of *detachment*. Of course it is bound to fail; not because there is no love in the marriage but simply because there is no real trust. Those of us who have married Rachels know the frustration of trying to get through their brick walls of detachment based on fear of rejection. Ultimately one of two things happens: either their partners capitulate, abandon any hope of 'getting through' and simply live off the starvation rations available in the relationship; or they call it a day and leave. The Rachel syndrome will have turned full-circle like a self-fulfilling prophecy: 'You see how right I was not to trust you; I knew you'd dump me one of these days – but at least I have the satisfaction of knowing that you never had all of me!' Thus Rachel sabotaged her marriage but entertained the fantasy that it was all her husband's fault.

This is one of the most familiar of death-dealing behaviour patterns in marriages. It arises out of the inner fears of a person which prove, ultimately, insurmountable. This represents one of the most sinister forms of 'marital insurance', withholding from the commitment, 'in case I get hurt'. What such people do not see is that they are in fact setting up themselves, and their partners, to fail.

The Ice Maiden syndrome

A variation of the Rachel syndrome is that of the Ice Maiden. This chilling phrase describes the person who resembles the Snow Queen in the fairy story.

A wicked imp once made a magic mirror, but the other imps were jealous and smashed it into thousands of tiny pieces. Some pieces fell into the eye and heart of a little boy named Kay and after that he was a changed person. He found fault with everything and everyone and even rejected his good friend Gerda. One day Kay was found by the Snow Queen who took him to her cold palace where he was turned into a block of ice. Gerda found out where Kay was being held and eventually made her way to the palace. She wrapped her arms around him but he was unmoved. As Gerda began to cry her warm tears melted the tiny pieces of the evil mirror in Kay's heart. He began to soften and recognizing Gerda he began to cry. His warm tears melted the tiny pieces of evil mirror in his eye and Kay was free again.

There are many people whose emotions appear to be frozen. They may be described as 'cold fish' or 'cold as ice'. They rarely display any kind of emotion; they remain cool and detached and distant. To some people, of course, these characteristics can be an attraction. At least such unemotional people are not going to pose a threat; they will not overwhelm others by their feelings. They will remain cool, calm and collected and always appear to be in control of themselves. Yet, like Kay in the Snow Queen's palace, they really do not have much option. Their feelings are not at their disposal. At one extreme, a classic feature of the criminal psychopath is the absence of any kind of feeling. They can maim, rape and mutilate without a twinge of conscience. They show no awareness of the enormity of their crimes and may even enjoy seeing others suffer. Thankfully not many of us go to that extreme, but it does alert us to one of the potential dangers of the person who is totally unfeeling. Most Ice Maidens remain coolly detached and those who fall in love with them spend tireless energy trying to 'get through' to them but without success. Whatever attraction their cool, calm and collected character once held, it soon evaporates. Because of the lack of emotional affirmation and response, the partners of Ice Maidens have a choice: either to stick it out and hope for the best, or leave and make a new life with a person who is more fully alive.

There is, of course, another side to the Ice Maiden syndrome. In terms of psychotherapy it would be vital to discover who the evil imps were in their personal history whose splinters of glass produced their frozen feelings. There may well have been appropriate reasons for learning how not to feel, especially if childhood traumatic feelings could not be processed but simply got buried. In the course of therapy over many years, I have witnessed the unfreezing of buried emotions and they emerge with the same pristine terror and rage in which they were first buried. The Ice Maidens (and 'Snow Men' too, since this is not a specifically feminine trait) can be helped but for many the risk is simply too great. They seek their happiness elsewhere, perhaps in intellectual pursuits or solitariness where they do not have to engage with other people at a deep intimate level.

When despairing partners decide to leave such people they almost inevitably experience feelings of guilt for doing so. This is one of the key experiences of this intermediate phase of separation. They often accuse themselves by playing the 'if only' game. Frankly such guilt is inappropriate, for in truth the unfreezing of buried emotions is a therapeutic task that taxes even the professionals in psychotherapy and psychoanalysis. Eventually you have a responsibility to yourself and that includes getting the

love you want and need. It is frequently the partners of
the frozen who come for counselling for it is they who
are feeling the tension and helplessness in their particular
ice palace called home. There is also the factor of blame,
because many such partners have come to believe that it
is *they* who are at fault. The lack of response – particularly
sexual response – by their partners is often attributed to a
variety of causes: I must be ugly, unattractive, sexually
impotent or frigid, unlovable, even repulsive. Such causes
are invariably found, upon deeper reflection, to be
unfounded.

But behind the icy façade of the Snow Man and the
Ice Maiden there is often an accurate awareness of the
implications of responding to the warmth of others. This
is contained in a poem given to me some years ago,
written by a man in the throes of the struggle between
his own inbuilt inhibitions and the passion of his lover. It
depicts the painful struggle between the Snowman and
the Firebird:

> It was a miracle of rare device
> A sunny pleasure dome with caves of ice . . .
> *Mais où sont les neiges d'antan?*
>
> Snowman strong in rigid cold
> In the winter of the world
> Crystal that you call your heart
> Westering sun can turn to gold
> Kindling fire without a spark:
> Fear true fire, be not too bold,
> Though you are young, your world is old!
>
> Firebird came and softly sang
> Of all the labile joys of Spring:
> 'Your heart upon the moment fling

I bring with me life and lust
Sparks to kindle gold I bring
So you in my love's flame shall trust!
Though you are old, my world is young,
Yearns for the safety of the strong!'

Her song beat swiftly on his ear
Resounding tympanies of fear.

Will he by will alone endure
The fearful turning of his year?

'Firebird, if you my heart enflame
You melt my heart – and all my frame
Quenching the flame that fires your blood:
Can your new Spring sustain the Flood?'

Firebirds and Snowmen are simply incompatible. Their
characteristics are totally inimical to one another and
although, as the poem movingly portrays, there are the
attractions that opposites often hold for one another, the
fundamental and psychological differences finally determine its outcome. The frozen emotions are an insurance
against ever getting hurt again. But they also keep out the
resources required for a healthy relationship.

However the breakdown of our marriage occurs, we
find ourselves having to face some unpalatable truths.
What are some of the key experiences we can expect in
this phase of leavetaking?

Key experiences

Anxiety
Events which threaten our peace and security as adults
have an uncanny knack of triggering off similar powerful

memories of our childhood. Then, the fear of abandonment, of being left alone at night, the lack of the presence of a strong parent-figure, would produce panic and anxiety in our childhood years. Many people going through the process of separation experience similar childish feelings. The first thing we need at this point is to remember that we are no longer children. We are not as weak or vulnerable or dependent as we once were.

Nevertheless there are normal adult feelings of anxiety that will accompany the process of leavetaking. If we are the partner who has left the matrimonial home, there may be anxiety about having done the right thing. We may experience self-doubt, self-recriminations and a lack of confidence about our decision. Depending upon our character, and how important 'doing the right thing' is for us, we can expect to experience anxiety about our future outside the marriage. If we have never lived alone this can raise enormous issues for us concerning our own ability to cope on our own. Our sleep pattern may be severely disrupted. We may be worrying about the rest of the family and how they are coping, and how to tell our parents and other family members. We may fear disapproval or condemnation.

If we are the partner who has been left, we too can experience anxiety. The degree to which we feel such anxiety will depend on a multitude of factors, not least our awareness of our self-confidence and the build-up (if any) to the final act of separation. One wife spoke of her fear of being left alone in the house at night, and having to take full responsibility for the three children for the first time in her life. She began to feel vulnerable and unprotected in the neighbourhood and entertained fantasies and fears of the house being broken into. Physical safety is a natural anxiety for some women, but men are also prone to such feelings. If they have been left with the children, for example, being thrown into a full-time mother/father role is full of worries. Simply knowing where things are, how the washing-machine works, and where clothes are kept may occupy a distraught father for some time. Getting into a new routine while keeping his job going at the same time causes endless anxiety for many fathers who find themselves alone. We are not 'going mad' when we experience anxiety; it is a natural part of the leavetaking process while we go through this transition process of living alone.

Isolation

There are three ways in which we can become isolated. These are social, psychological and physical.

The physical isolation – of becoming one instead of one of a pair – is often a weird feeling. Depending on how long we have been together, there has been a constant understanding of 'us' and 'we'. Now there is only me and I. The lack of adult company can be almost painful at times, and for those who have never learned to like and enjoy their own company there is often a long period of painful adjustment. The house seems empty, there is no one to talk to, we are alone.

Secondly, however, there is the psychological isolation. By this I mean those feelings that we may have that tell us that we are utterly alone in the world, that no one cares a damn, and that no one understands how it is for us right now. Our world seems totally closed to outsiders. How can anyone know how it feels to be in my shoes? And all the time we may be keeping up the pretence that everything is all right and we're feeling fine. We may even begin to rationalize the situation and tell ourselves how lucky we are that our partner has gone and left us in peace. But the reality, in the privacy of our inner world, is just the reverse.

Thirdly, there is the question of social isolation. Some of this may well be self-imposed as we try and keep ourselves to ourselves for a while. But there will be some people who may avoid us for a variety of reasons. Some will not want to intrude into our private grief; others simply will not know what to say. Like a death in the family, people simply keep away out of a sense of their own inadequacy. We may experience the rejection by some of our family, especially the family of our former partner. Former friends and acquaintances may quietly disappear – 'not wishing to take sides' – but in reality feeling embarrassed and not wanting to get involved. If only they knew the additional pain such calculated avoidance can inflict, then perhaps fewer would do it.

The most important thing to do in this period of feeling isolated is to *tell someone what has happened*. Don't suffer in silence. Ask a friend or family member, whom you trust not to lecture you or give you good advice, just to come and listen to your story. You do not need 'approval', merely understanding. You may find it useful to consult a counsellor or ask for an appointment at your local RELATE office. At all costs, avoid shutting yourself away; problems can get distorted that way and in any case it's unhealthy.

Pain

Whether or not it is we who do the separating, pain – both physical and mental – frequently comes to the fore during this intermediate phase of leavetaking. I recall my own chest pain which lasted for about a year; I couldn't take a deep breath without feeling pain. I did seek reassurance from my doctor that there was nothing organically wrong, and then settled down to wait until it eventually passed. In my own case it was, I believe, a mixture of anxiety and grief. I needed to cry often just to relieve the mounting feelings associated with my leaving home. However right the decision to leave may be, many people experience feelings of pain both physical and psycho-logical.

Depression
This is one classic way in which the pain involved in leavetaking can come out. We get depressed. If we have a history of depression then this will come as no surprise to us. Our feelings will be more than justified. But if we have no prior experience of real, clinical depression then we can be taken by surprise by this new experience. In either case it would be as well to consult your GP, informing them of the situation you are going through and seeking their advice.

Those of you who find it hard to admit to your own limitations may be reluctant to go to ask for anyone's help. But if ever you were justified in seeking help it is during the breakdown of a marriage. Think of all those you have sat and listened to for hours when their marriage broke down! Depression is largely caused through the habitual bottling-up of genuine emotions. Some of us have made it into an art form, indeed we may have boasted that we never share our feelings with anyone. Two familiar emotions are guilt and anger.

Guilt
This is frequently associated with the partner who leaves the family home, but it is by no means exclusively so. Either partner can experience guilt depending upon how aware they are of what is going on inside them. While it is true that some people manage to keep all awareness of feelings tightly shut, others will begin to 'feel bad' about their part in the separation. Circumstances may determine the appropriateness of our guilty feelings, and whether or

not we have made enough effort to be open about our intentions. To the extent that we have been economical with the truth with our partner then our guilt may be appropriate.

Those who leave their partner to live with someone else often find that this experience of guilt can lead to the 'Yo-Yo syndrome' (see p. 57f.). In order to salve our guilty conscience we return to the family home, only to feel guilty about the lover we have now abandoned. Some people then embark on a 'shuttle diplomacy' trying to get everyone to feel all right. Such ambition is fatally flawed. Someone is going to feel hurt no matter what they do. Accepting responsibility for our part in the breakdown of the marriage is one way to process this guilt and need not lead to a lifetime of personal self-reproach.

Anger

There are very few separations in which anger does not play a part from time to time. It is a perfectly normal emotion and, if we are to avoid the worst excesses of depression, needs appropriate expression. Depending upon the circumstances of our separation we may have had the chance of letting off steam to our partner some time ago. But angry feelings will continue to arise and will not be over and done with all at once. They will come and go depending on either our mood or upon our changing circumstances. When we feel our partner is being uncooperative, or when we are short of money, or people are avoiding us, we will feel anger rising up and we are then tempted to play the 'blaming game', believing that this is all 'their' fault. Life isn't fair at times, and we are entitled to say so.

Survival plans

Whether we are the one who is leaving or the one left behind, we shall need some kind of survival plan to cover the immediate experience of separation. In cases where the separation has been planned for some time, this will nearly always have the chance of being in place prior to the actual separation. Some couples will have sat down and discussed how things are to be divided up, what financial arrangements seem fair to both parties, visiting and access to the children and other matters of practical concern. In other cases, where sudden and unexpected departure has occurred and there is no such luxury as an orderly withdrawal, other issues then arise.

Finance may be the uppermost issue. The payment of mortgage and household bills will probably be the most pressing of our concerns. It is the accepted custom these days to inform the appropriate authorities of our changed situation and ask for a 'cooling-off period' while we clarify our likely income.

Is this separation a temporary 'blip' or is it permanent? Will he or she be back in a few days' time, or is it more serious than we think? Whatever the outcome is likely to be, we need help immediately, and this is where trusted friends or family members can assist in many of the practical issues we are now facing. We may have to pocket our pride in order to ask for help, but it may be better than suffering in silence.

We shall soon find ourselves entering a third phase of leavetaking and the more thoroughly we have worked through the key experiences of this second phase the more prepared we will be for the period of consolidation.

7. The Four Phases of Marital Break-Up

III THE CONSOLIDATION PHASE

Our society expects everyone to get married. Social life, whether public or private, is organized around the married couple. The romantic dyad is the archetypal relationship in our culture, and those who do not 'pair off' in some legal and definitive sense are still regarded as 'defectors' in a Noah's Ark culture. Especially if one is over thirty, there is always a suspected reason for sustained singlehood: one is a misanthrope or libertine, a closet homosexual, or hopelessly repressed.

(Madonna Kolbenschlag)[30]

Like other models of the process of grief, leavetaking too follows a fairly predictable pattern which the passing of time seems to structure for us. Of course, 'phases' are an invention of the map-maker; marital cartographers are nowhere as scientific as their terrestrial counterparts. Nevertheless this third phase does exist in reality and can occur anywhere from a few weeks after the separation to several months.

I have called this period consolidation because (in the ideal at least) it builds upon the gains of the previous two phases. I believe that if differs quite markedly from the breaking down and breaking out phases, for in this third phase we are 'breaking in' (like a new pair of shoes) an entirely different experience of life.

The biggest difference will be the experience of singleness.

Singleness

I am using the word 'single' in its experiential, not its legal, form. Although the facts are that you may still be married, even though separated, the feelings are those of the single person. By the time most marriages break down we have forgotten what being single feels like. We may experience this awareness with some fear and anxiety since we have existed as a twosome for so long that it has become part of a way of life.

There are many ways in which this awareness will surface. A sense of strangeness will almost certainly be experienced from time to time. We turn to our partner to comment on something on TV and their chair is empty; we awake at night with a panic of being alone; we may whistle or shout our usual greeting on entering the family home, only to be met with a deafening silence; their car is not in the drive. So many ways in which the reality of separation forces itself upon us.

This reality is one of the ways in which we are being taught how to be single again. Being single *again* is a totally different experience from the first time we were single. We have aged, for one thing, and it is likely that we have children for another. I am not using the word single to denote 'on the marriage market' but merely to draw attention to the necessity of both recognizing and negotiating this important aspect of separation.

During our marriage we have simply got used to living as a pair. This means, among other things, thinking as a couple. We learn one another's likes and dislikes, we make allowances for the other partner, we share our space together. We are and feel accountable to one another in terms of our time and resources. We take their preferences into account and we make all the usual compromises familiar in the marriage partnership. Within the warmth and intimacy of a loving relationship, all these accommodations to being a couple are more than worthwhile. When we marry there is a certain surrender of some of our autonomy and space in the interests of the relationship and for most of the time we feel that such investment is not only necessary but more than rewarded by the resulting acceptance and enjoyment of love.

So becoming single again means putting all this into reverse. The autonomy once more becomes absolute, not relative. We have all the space we want – enough to drown in sometimes. There are no more compromises to the needs of the other person, no more thinking as a couple. For most of us going through such a process, it can become a weird world. No wonder people speak of it as a *dismemberment*, like losing an arm or 'our other half'. Like losing a partner through death, we enter the demi-world of finding ourselves alone and making all the kinds of adjustments in order to recreate the world around our singleness.

How do we do this? Most of us facing singleness after a long marriage are hardly conscious that we are 'going through a phase'. Getting through each day is struggle enough. I recall the entire loss of structure to my day, hence my need for a daily schedule in order to replace what had been lost. However much the relationship may have been deteriorating, our partner's comings and goings at least provided some shape and form to our lives. We were probably having to take into account their presence, however painful, in a reactive way. Yet there is all the difference in the world when we are faced with being pro-active rather than reactive to the movements of others. It was this shapelessness to my day that I found so threatening and hard to come to terms with. Not all of us, of course, lose their jobs at the same time as losing their partner, but when these two experiences come together there are, I believe, additional problems to come to terms with, like disorientation and formlessness.

And there is no one to share all this with. If we are left with children, there is the natural temptation to use them as dumping grounds for our mounting frustration and loneliness. Older teenage children may well have the capacity to understand and accept this from us, while the younger ones will find it unintelligible. We may turn to parents for a listening ear or to friends and neighbours. While we may give the impression that we want them to solve our problems, and thereby frighten some away when they feel helpless, what we need most of all is some acceptance and understanding of how we feel at this stage of the separation. It is at this point that we may encounter the perennial problem of being thought of as a threat to the marriages of others. Like some latter-day leper, our same-sex friends may think of us as rivals, and therefore in order to protect their marriage (and their spouses) prefer to distance themselves from us. We may find ourselves carrying their fearful projections that in some way we are going to infect their own relationship or at least pose a challenge since we are thought of as footloose and fancy-free. Excuses are made, distances maintained, their diaries become mysteriously filled with more urgent things and we become frighteningly aware that we are more alone than ever. This becomes an additional twist in our saga of separation.

While the journey of returning to singleness can be extremely painful, finding a way through is an asset that we take into our future. Once through, singleness and the sometimes paralysing aloneness we feel can never again return to threaten us in the same way. Like all other rites of passage, we can never return to the previous stage where singleness threatened our very existence: we are out; we are through. It is an asset precisely because we are able to make choices about our future and especially about future life-partners free from the urgency and desperation born not out of love but out of fear of being alone.

Michael came to see me recently after a particularly hair-raising separation and divorce. He was under pressure from his new girlfriend to make a permanent commitment which he felt he was unable to do. He had deep wounds from the vicious way in which his wife left him and her subsequent manic behaviour towards him, and felt that honesty with his new woman was the correct way forward. On examination, it appeared that the pressure for him to 'make up his mind' came not from any prevarication on his part, but from his girlfriend's need to leave her parental home where she had lodged since her own separation. Here was a disaster in the making, where part of his attractiveness was that he could supply an instant 'key of the door' to her problems. While *she* saw this as his problem ('Why don't you make a commitment and ask me to live with you?') *he* saw it as her problem ('Why don't you move out and live on your own for a while?'). In this way we can clearly see the differing motives involved in this period of singleness; sometimes the fear of living on our own can force us into unwise and ultimately destructive demands or choices.

Marcus found coping with singleness painful in the extreme. He soon fell madly in love with Anne who seemed to offer him all he dreamed of. In proposing marriage to her it never crossed his mind that she would refuse. But refuse she did. Her words are worth bearing in mind. She said, 'Marcus, I love you too, but I refuse to be the key to get you out of your box!' Marcus thought they were the cruellest words he had ever heard and felt deeply rejected. Years later he came to see the wisdom and indeed the love behind them. For Anne was able to discern what Marcus, in his pain and loneliness, could not see: his desire for her was both distorted and confused by his deeper need to avoid the implications of his singleness. Unfortunately for many people, they lack this wisdom and make precipitate decisions that they rue in the years to come. So often our short-term need for a mate exceeds our need to make a more cautious and long-term decision about our future. This need to hang on to significant others is, of course, one way in which a far more important issue comes to light: what to do with the partner from whom we are now separated?

Hanging on and letting go

This consolidation phase has yet another task which will call for our careful attention in due course: how can I let him or her go?

In one sense, of course, they *have* gone – or we have! There is an actual separation to come to terms with but, consistent with our death-denying culture, we sometimes play games with ourselves and pretend that there will be a return and a second chance. It is one way in which we so often avoid the grief involved when couples part. Should the longed-for rapprochement not take place, we can pretend that it is only a matter of time. Life then goes on 'hold'; no decisions are made about our future 'in case he or she comes back'. I heard of a woman recently whose husband had walked out over twenty years ago (a 'Dear Jane' syndrome), left everything behind him, changed his name (and religion), went to Canada, married and now has a family. Yet there is still the belief within that abandoned wife that he will come back. While there are male friendships, they are all platonic, and her friends cannot understand why her life is still on 'hold' in the absence of even a shred of encouragement that her former husband will return!

There is a common desire to deny the separation because in that way we can deny the pain we feel. The ways in which some people fool themselves into thinking about the return of their spouse are many and sometimes devious. In some cases there is a real danger of abandoned spouses disappearing into 'cloud-cuckoo land', indulging in childish magical thinking that very often leads to serious thought disorders.

Every relationship has its history. The difficult thing to do, for some people, is to hold on to what was good and constructive in the marriage relationship while learning eventually to let go of the other person involved in the marital history. For me, this question revolved around what to do with my wedding anniversary each year. We had usually marked the day in some way or other as important and significant for us both, and it seemed odd in the extreme when the first anniversary after we separated came round. Going out for dinner together did not seem the most appropriate thing to suggest! Were there anniversary cards in the shops with black edges to commemorate the demise of the marriage? And – while we are mentioning leavetaking rituals – why are there none when a marriage dies? The eventual divorce notification will hardly do as a substitute for or equivalent of an anniversary card! I talked this over with some friends, and they suggested using the anniversary day as a celebration of our children. So each 3 April I used to write to my four daughters until the need to do so passed with time, and the letting go process was as complete as it ever can be.

That last sentence seems to me to contain an important truth: 'As complete as it ever can be' means that we need not look for a total blotting-out of our previous relationship. Not only is this impossible but it is also undesirable for a number of reasons. First, we have a need to keep in touch with the reality of our experiences, however sadly they may end. Secondly, we need to hold on to the good and worthwhile parts of that experience and not fall into the temptation to deny there was anything good in it. I once told my ex-wife that our marriage had been hell; what I think I meant was that that was how it felt when I said it, but of course a more objective assessment made this statement far from true. Thirdly, we need to recognize the changes that occurred in either our spouse or ourselves that finally led to the break-up of the marriage. I have written elsewhere[31] about the danger of unilateral change within a significant relationship, and how such change need not necessarily be threatening. But, of course, it is often the case that our needs change, or our awareness changes, or we decide to put our foot down about some negative aspect of the marriage and then the whole relationship can come tumbling down about our ears. Given these factors, it is important to recognize that the letting go process is never totally complete. Where there are children to the marriage, this is even more obvious. Their own life crises and especially the arrival of the grand-children mean that *both* parents are likely to want to be involved in the subsequent celebrations and this can be the cause of a good deal of heart-searching when we are confronted by our 'ex'!

So our matrimonial leavetaking is rarely total. It is usually a relative experience. Memories, for one thing, keep coming back; and the family photograph album is a challenge to our ability to cope with the separation. Can we even bear to look at it? Since all couples have their own particular histories, no one model can possibly apply to all. It appears easier for some people than others to let go of their former spouse and that will depend upon a multitude of factors: length of the relationship, age, financial issues, payment of maintenance, other relationships, proximity of the partners after separation, needs of the children and access to them by both parents, and so on.

Key experiences

In this third consolidation phase there are at least three key experiences to encounter.

Growing confidence

By the time we enter and negotiate the third phase of leavetaking we have *survived*! Our initial fears have been worked through and, much to our surprise and sometimes that of other people, we have not gone mad, emigrated, or committed suicide. This can lead to a necessary growth of confidence in our own resources and for many people it is a period of new discovery about themselves.

If we entered the breaking down phase with fear and trepidation, and the breaking out phase with anxiety, depression and anger, we may find ourselves at the end of the breaking in phase in a far stronger situation than we could ever have imagined. It is in this important phase that we discover inner strengths and powers, and hidden or denied aspects of ourself that have come to our rescue. Instead of our 'I'll-never-cope!' script we had at the beginning of the leavetaking process we can now place a very firm 'I can cope!' We have in fact learned something about ourselves that apart from the process of leavetaking we may never have learned: *we are not as powerless as we thought we were.* Men who wondered how they could cope with the complexity of the washing-machine or domestic arrangements discover that they can learn about such things, and sometimes get job satisfaction in the doing of them. Women who fancy they cannot understand the running of the bank account or what to do when the septic tank is full, discover that it only takes a little application to manage such fearful possibilities. As we do, we receive fresh resources of confidence about our ability to cope on our own and this can give rise to the discovery of more of our human potential. Iris would never learn to drive, protesting that she lacked confidence. When she married Alf, fifteen years her senior, she realized that she was likely to be isolated in her small village should anything happen to him. So Iris took driving lessons and passed at her third attempt. She would never have made that discovery had she remained in her first marriage.

Henri Nouwen, in *The Living Reminder*, states that it is only when we leave that others who have been depending on us receive the space to grow into their own potential.[32] Like Iris, they are able to make alternative choices to those they made within their first marriage. Take the case of Robert Raines:

> When I left home Peg had my paternal umbrella removed and was free for the first time in twenty-three years to imagine, design and construct her own life. She took charge. Several years later, she is remarried, a Ph.D. candidate in the field of counselling,

and by her own account more happy and fulfilled than ever before.[33]

It is this ability to take charge of our own lives once more and to revise our ideas of dependency and inadequacy that this third phase of consolidation puts before us. And not until we reach this phase in our leavetaking process are we able to hear that such discoveries lie within our reach. If we are told this at an earlier stage, the chances are that we will not even *hear* what other people are saying to us. We would be too close to the event of separation, too aware of our own inner panic and pain, to entertain such lofty hopes that somehow we will come through this a different and more capable person. All of us have within us hidden resources and undiscovered talents that somehow fail to get into the blood-stream of our marriages. We have the ability to think differently about ourselves freed from the predisposing factors of our former partner. Such factors can often cripple and restrain us, and help to form a distorted image of who we truly are. People who have been consistently put down by their former partners have the opportunity of revising the definition handed to them: ugly, useless, stupid spouses are often discovering their beauty, power and abilities only after the break-up of their marriage and they are removed from the toxic effect of their partner's projections.

'Awful cooks' find that others enjoy their cooking. 'Useless fathers' discover hidden parental talents. Husbands and wives who have been accused of being 'no good in bed' can be helped to discover their full sexual potential within the new framework of a caring and supportive relationship. 'Losers' can become 'winners'.

Sometimes when this occurs we become aware of another key factor in this phase.

Familiarity with a new reality

Paul Tillich once wrote, 'The new comes not out of the old but out of the *death* of the old.'[34] This is an important truth to grasp as we negotiate the breaking in period of the new reality which each separation brings with it. The new reality is not just a continuation of the old life we once lived with our former partner. Sooner or later there must come a real break with the old way of doing and thinking and behaving while we were in the former relationship.

We need to negotiate what may be the biggest transition of our lives – uncoupling from our former partners. It is as well that we have the difficulties clearly located on our leavetaking map:

1. The temptation to deny the new reality:
   She/he'll come back soon
   This break is only temporary
   She/he couldn't do this to the kids
   He knows how much I need him
   (*Hidden message: This isn't happening to me*)

2. The tendency to emphasize our helplessness:
   I'll never be able to manage
   I so depend upon him/her
   I'm falling to pieces
   How can I cope with this?
   (*Hidden message: I'm useless just as she/he said I was!*)

3. The need to become ill:
   This separation is driving me mad
   My migraines have come back
   I must go to the doctor
   (*Hidden message: Being ill is one way to attract attention*)

4. The desire to shift the blame to our partner:
    It's all his fault!
    He never was any good
    The ungrateful bitch!
    (*Hidden message: I've never learned how to take responsibility for my life*)

5. The vow never to trust anyone ever again:
    My mother told me not to trust him!
    That's women for you!
    I'm finished with men!
    (*Hidden message: I can't cope with pain*)

6. The flight into a new relationship:
    I'm entitled to some enjoyment, aren't I?
    It's only for some company
    I can't stand being on my own
    (*Hidden message: I'm incomplete without another person*)

7. The escape into drink and depression:
    What else is there to do?
    At least this way I can forget
    Oblivion's better than pain
    I'll kill myself!
    (*Hidden message: Look what you've done to me*)

These are some of the more familiar obstacles standing in the way of those who struggle to come to terms with the 'life after marriage' syndrome. Most of us try at least one and maybe all of these escape routes in our bid to avoid the pain and the hardship involved in accepting that the old partnership is dead. It is also desirable that we discover some or all of the hidden messages that fuel and stimulate such destructive attitudes towards ourselves. Before we can negotiate the new reality we have to let go of the old reality – that's the rub.

For there is nothing magical or automatic about finding for ourselves a new life after the separation. It doesn't just happen: it has to be worked for. The temptation to take refuge in the 'Little Bo-Peep' syndrome ('Leave them alone and they'll come home, wagging their tails behind them') must be resisted. Neither is it just a matter of time. Time, of course, is the stream in which these changes take place, but time alone is no healer. What we *do* with the time after our separation is all-important. If we take refuge in a permanent dependency on drugs, alcohol or someone else's bed we are merely prolonging the agony. It is at this point that our decision-making becomes important.

Making decisions for ourselves is not something we feel able to do in the immediate phase. We are too numb and shocked. But eventually we have to make some decisions about our future, even if it is to be merely short-term. *It is in the process of making decisions that we come to accept the new reality.* For by this process we are establishing and exercising our individual autonomy: the power to determine our own future. In the past such decisions may have been made either for us by our partner or in conjunction with them. Now we have no need to check things out with him or her. We are free to make our own choices about everything from wallpaper to newspapers, from cereals to soap operas and from the time you go to bed to the time you get up. Gradually such choices become second nature and the temptation to turn to our (now absent) partner and ask their advice or approval disappears.

Fresh bouts of grief or anger
Breaking into this new reality does not mean that we are totally free of our past. It is here that we occasionally get

tripped up by the factor mentioned earlier: the need to negotiate the leavetaking process so as to make it 'as complete as it ever can be'. For there will be the odd occasions when we regress into feelings more appropriate to former phases of the leavetaking process. Fresh bouts of grief or anger may overwhelm us from time to time, and this is perfectly normal given the circumstances. In times of elation or crisis – times historically shared with our former mate – we may miss not turning to share such moments with them. It is then that the full reality of our new situation hits us with sometimes an almost physical force. I remember one such moment when our first grandchild was born. It was extremely odd to find myself visiting my daughter in hospital alone – when everything in me felt that both parents ought to have been present to share in the joy of Emily's birth. Grief and anger can be very closely related at such moments. When former spouses start playing the power-games associated with some separations ('I want to be told first!') then such feelings can re-emerge from a place within us which we thought of as empty.

Other moments may arise upon the choices of our children. We may feel that our former spouse is preferred to ourselves, or that they think we are not doing a good job in our task of being single parents. The 'Santa Claus Saturday father' syndrome comes to mind. While she is scrimping and saving to make ends meet during the week, it is galling in the extreme to find the children arriving home from their day with dad piled high with (to our way of thinking at least) unnecessary luxuries, especially when he has failed to pay the family maintenance for the past few weeks! Anger can get projected on to the children and new problems arise within our depleted family unit. Such occurrences form part of the new reality and we need to discover more appropriate ways of dealing with them. The proper grievance needs to be directed to the husband who is failing to meet his responsibilities towards the separated family, or to the courts where such payments can be enforced. The truth can finally dawn upon us: we can cope, we have the power to do so, and we can at last take responsibility for what we allow others to do to us.

As we negotiate this third phase in our leavetaking map we are in fact making important preparations for the fourth and final phase, 'breaking through'.

8. The Four Phases of Marital Break-up

IV   THE FUTURE PHASE

My beloved spake, and said unto me,
Rise up, my love, my fair one, and come away.
For, lo, the winter is past,
The rain is over and gone;
The flowers appear on the earth;
The time of the singing of birds is come,
And the voice of the turtle is heard in our land;
The fig tree putteth forth her green figs,
And the vines with the tender grape
Give a good smell.
Arise, my love, my fair one, and come away.

(*The Song of Solomon* 2:10–13 AV)

This final part of our leavetaking map concerns our future which by definition is open-ended. Perhaps at the beginning, at any rate, it will be largely unknown. I call the process involved in this phase 'breaking through'.

I am painfully aware that some readers have not yet negotiated the previous phases. You may indeed still be in the aftermath of the initial shock of the separation. However, I feel it would be valuable for you to spare the time reading this chapter in order to keep before you the possibility of your coming through the crisis intact, however unlikely or distant a possibility that may seem. As mentioned before, in the second phase of leavetaking I was immensely moved by Robert Raines's book, *Going Home*, and encouraged that someone who had been through what I was going through had survived. There is no reason why you should not do the same.

Others of you are approaching the final phase of your leavetaking and also wanting assurance that this can be a creative time for you. I was encouraged by the title of Mel Krantzler's book, *Creative Divorce*,[35] as a sign that there can be life after divorce. This emphasis needs to be made at a time when, for many people, divorce is always and necessarily considered to be a bad thing, a destructive thing, a thing to be avoided at all costs. This is due partly to their ignorance of the fact that divorce – and, yes, eventually the death of our spouse – can be a liberating experience. Liberating, yet painful in achieving that liberation. That is my conviction in writing this book, that we *can* find the 'good' in our goodbyes. My conviction comes out of my experience that, tackled creatively, even the most painful of separations can lead on to an increase of happiness and the fulfilment of our human potential. To deny this would be to deny the experience of thousands of people each year who make the breakthrough into a new and exciting life.

Key experiences

At least five key experiences feature in the fourth and final phase of our leavetaking map.

Hope

This is a delicate human plant, and hard to keep alive during the cold winds of separation and divorce. Despair and depression seem the greater realities at the beginning of that process. Yet by the time we reach the fourth and final phase of leavetaking it begins to thrive again, and we start to look forward to a future containing happiness and real life.

The signs of hope are, by now, all around us. First and most important, we have survived! All the earlier fears and misgivings, and much of the pain, are now behind us and we can start to remake our world. Secondly we can give ourselves the credit we deserve for having made the creative changes necessary to negotiating the leavetaking process. We have taken risks, we have made changes, we have shown determination and courage, and we have broken through the claustrophobic fear of failure. Thirdly we have found the hidden reserves and resources within ourselves which we never thought were there. 'Fancy me changing a three-pin plug!' we may say. Fourthly we begin to measure the distance we have travelled since those traumatic first days of the separation. We begin to see the failure of the previous relationship in a perspective of time and can trace more accurately the predisposing causes of that failure. Fifthly we have discovered a 'new me', hitherto concealed by the shape and content of the old relationship. Those parts of ourselves that we either consciously or, more likely, unconsciously buried in the interests of the old relationship we have uncovered and find that we like ourselves better this way.

All these factors increase our ability to hope and to plan for our new future. We may have discovered others who, like ourselves, have survived the trauma of separation or abandonment and are planning new and exciting things for their future. Where were all these survivors when we thought we could never make it, we may ask ourselves? The truth is that they were there all the time only we never noticed them. The pain and the hurt were too present and too real for us to pay them any attention. We never thought we would survive anyway, so why bother? But now we see how that thought-process was but part of our grieving process. We can't look on the bright side until we have encountered the dark side. We also discover who our true friends have been all along, especially those who would not allow us to wallow in self-pity and who loved us enough to keep us within the realms of honesty and truth about our situation. We may not have thanked them at the time, but eventually we may discover how right they were to believe in us when our self-respect and all hope seemed to have been lost. I am now grateful to all those friends who reminded me of the choices I had made about my own separation, but I am sure at the time I experienced some of their honest remarks as uncaring and even unsympathetic. I had to learn the hard lesson mentioned by Scott Peck: 'Problems do not go away. They must be worked through or else they remain, for ever a barrier to the growth and development of spirit.'[36]

The need to share

It is not until we leave one relationship that we feel free to form others. I look back to my own period of living alone, in Rugby, in Chicago and later in Aylesbury, as an important and formative period of my life. It was more than three years from the decision to separate to my second marriage in August 1982. I am glad of those three years living as a single person and I see them as a kind of school for personal development since within them I did a lot of growing up, and a lot of growing out of former destructive attitudes towards myself. What I discovered was that I had to learn to be more caring about myself if

I was ever to be able to contribute to a future loving relationship. For I was aware of my need to share my life and my love with another, but knew that I first had to get through the process of leavetaking. I was well aware that I could not say Hallo until I had said Goodbye to my former marriage and the time I spent doing that was well worthwhile. By 1982 I had come to terms with the past, and could begin to plan a new future with Jan.

A big difference I noticed was that the desperation for someone – anyone – to fill the gap left by my separation had gone. I now realize that such desperation was born more out of fear of not being able to survive the loneliness and less out of the desire for them as a person. I had still to learn the lesson discovered much later in my journey: 'Treating ourselves like appliances that can be unplugged and plugged in again at will or cars that stop and start with the twist of a key, we have forgotten the importance of fallow time and winter and rests in music.'[37] It would have been so easy to 'plug in' to a new relationship in order to escape the fear and the pain of being alone, and it was not until I learned that I was not an appliance, and that I had resources for survival *within myself* that this manic search ended. It was easier for people to relate to me once I had given up my mollusc-like need for attachment.

I also gradually realized that the need to share my life with another person was an entirely different pursuit from the need for someone to attach myself to. Sharing had to do with growth and loving awareness; attaching had to do with an infantile need for dependency and lack of autonomy. Sharing meant opening myself to the truth of the other; attaching had more to do with closing off truth and reality and blindly surrendering my autonomy to the vicissitudes of the other. Sharing meant I had something to give; attaching was merely a display of my need to receive. Sharing meant recognizing my worthwhileness and my ability both to give and receive; attaching meant staying with my chronic sense of inferiority and worthlessness. Sharing meant celebrating my self with an other; attaching meant apologizing for my existence. Sharing meant freedom; attaching meant slavery.

I have come to realize that this crucial distinction lies somewhere near the heart of the reason why so many second marriages fail. Like parasites, we desire not a partner but a host on whom we can feed. Leech-like, we perceive our partners as the sole means of our survival. The subsequent relationship may be compared to other life-giving attachments, like umbilical cords through which we receive nourishment and sustenance. For the unborn child such attachments are natural and necessary, and it would appear that many of us carry a subconscious fantasy that we are still in this inter-uterine condition. Clearly a 'new birth' is needed by which we cut the cord and discover that, in spite of our fears of annihilation, we have lungs – and can survive on our own. We are able to become separate beings who need now to share ourselves with others, not become attached in a desperation born of fear.

I stress this aspect of leavetaking since it seems to me vital in our search for future happiness. If for no other reason, the successful negotiation of this part of our journey into the future means that we are free to be ourselves. Attachment, on the other hand, leads remorsely into possessiveness, that unhealthy clinging that speaks more of infantile dependency than healthy love. This desire to possess the other in turn leads into jealousy, the frantic whirlwind of suspicion and imagined rivals who threaten to remove our possession from us. The constant need for reassurance that springs from jealousy depletes the energy and resources of the partner who feels eternally under suspicion. The childish plea, 'You really do love me, don't you?' is more likely to remove whatever love is left than reinforce it. What may have started out as a comfortable feeling of being needed by their partner ends up as a desperate struggle to be free from the stranglehold of those blood-sucking tendrils. Love is never possession.

The ability to risk new relationships

This will depend largely on our past experience and the depth of the pain and hurt we suffered during and after the separation. If we feel our wounds are slight – a mere graze – risking other relationships may seem no big deal. But if we have been deeply scarred by our former mate then we will necessarily – and sensibly – take more time to recover our confidence. Before we contemplate taking the risk of a new relationship, there is one thing above all others that will inspire such confidence. It may be put in the form of a credal formula: *Never again will I allow others to dominate me, define me or dump on me*. In other words, we are not the same person who went into that previous relationship, since we have grown up and abandoned those stifling and self-destructive opinions we held about ourself.

Domination is how we defeat ourselves by allowing others to exercise all the power in the relationship. Of course, being human, there is always a pay-off for allowing this state of affairs to continue, since we can then hand them all the responsibility for sorting things out! But growing up means growing out of the need for such rewards when we discover it is more appropriate to take adult responsibility for our lives. We can only get into a safe place to take risks about new relationships when we discover our previous, devious ways of relating and abandon them.

Allowing others to define who we are also needs to be

changed. In many subtle ways we can influence the way
our partners see themselves, for good or for ill. Many
people suffer 'death by a thousand cuts', no single cut of
any importance but in an accumulative way they sap all
the self-esteem from us. Constant putting down of a
spouse has become an art form in some marriages. 'Do
put your clothes on – you're no oil painting!' may at first
appear humorous but those words, repeated over a long
marriage, were enough to remove every vestige of sexual
confidence for one spouse. Shame, guilt, self-doubt,
gradually began to take their toll, until in the end he
wondered if he could possibly be gay! (What he did not
understand until later was that he was carrying his wife's
own guilt and shame about sex that she had dumped on
him. More on this below.) It took a lot of guts for him
to work this through in his therapy and ultimately to risk
a full sexual experience with a liberated woman who could
affirm his masculinity and genital loveliness and power.
He had, albeit unknowingly, allowed his wife to define
him as weak, ugly and sexually impotent. After his own
liberation he would never allow anyone to instill such
doubts in him again.

This theme of discovering our true identity is the theme
of *Do I Have to Give Up ME to be Loved by YOU?* already
referred to, in which Jordan and Margaret Paul write:
'Answering "No" creates a most unusual relationship –
what we call an Evolving Relationship. In an Evolving
Relationship partners engage in a process that leads to
individual freedom and integrity while increasing intimacy. To get there, partners have to become vulnerable
and take emotional risks.'[38] It is only in this fourth and
final phase of leavetaking that we feel free enough to take
such risks.

We must never again allow others to dump their stuff
on us. What stuff? Well, the kind of stuff referred to above

– *her* sexual hang-ups dumped on *him*. The reasons are not hard to find. If I make you the weak one I don't have to look at my own weakness. If I dump my hang-ups on you I don't have to take responsibility for doing anything about them. It then becomes your problem. Countless spouses, when they come to unpack the Left Luggage from their former marriages, discover to their surprise and anger just how much they 'took' from their partner. I don't just mean taking other people for granted but a far more sinister (and less obvious) pattern of behaviour which actually distorts our self-identity and damages it. Tim never forgot the moment when he made such a discovery concerning what he had allowed his ex-wife to dump on him. He was at a party with some of his work colleagues enjoying the disco when a woman with whom he was dancing exclaimed, 'Tim, are you aware of your sexual energy right now?' Among some corny 'come-ons' this may be rated highly, and yet Tim correctly heard the meaning of the message and it shook him enough to take it seriously. For that is not how he would ever have defined himself, yet here was someone who knew him in a work context commenting on her perception of an attribute which Tim had never discovered: he was sexually attractive! Slowly he began to emerge from his prevailing mood of 'down in the dumps'. He recognized, like many others, that dumps are places for rubbish, not people. He decided not to stay there any longer and this began a long process of taking a hard look at what else was happening in his marriage.

This credo, therefore, is of crucial importance for our future happiness and our ability to relate creatively to others. The life-long habits of being dominated by others, allowing others to define who we are and dump their own stuff on us need to be deliberately and consciously abandoned. There is no alternative if we are to make a new future as opposed to a stale repetition of the past. We will not risk future relationships if we have not dealt with the Left Luggage of the old ones. The reason is not hard to find.

Having been hurt (rejected, humiliated, diminished) in our former relationship we become limited in our ability to risk new relationships. An old, battered self is not much to offer anyone. Hence the Ugly Duckling pattern of thought: 'Who'd give me a second look?' We can be helped to discover that we are really swans, but only by looking into the lake of someone else's eyes. As Tim discovered, others perceive us differently and it is this difference in attitude towards ourselves that empowers us to take risks for our future happiness.

Risks do not have to be foolhardy, however. We do not have to believe everyone, trust everyone, or think that everyone will have our best interests at heart. Risk-taking is related to our ability to survive; the greater that ability the greater risk we may take. Second marriages would not be half as much at risk as they are (statistically) if only they were undertaken by those who discovered their own value, power and ability to survive independently of others. This process is inseparable from our ability not only to love others but to love ourselves as well.

The need to be loved
Much heated debate continues about what at first sight may appear to be a truism: that in order to love someone else we must first love ourselves. Yet this statement contains within it revolutionary elements we need to examine. One writer sums it up thus: 'How could we love, how could we give, how could we trust, how could we share what we didn't have to give? If we did not spend some time creating ourselves in depth and power, with what were we going to relate to others?'[39]

As Mel Krantzler reminds us, 'Self-love . . . is the soil in which these other kinds of love flourish.'[40] The reasons are not hard to find.

At birth – indeed, for those who take pregnancies more seriously these days, from conception itself – the developing baby has a need of affirmation and acceptance. It is not often difficult to love a newborn child in all its helplessness and vulnerability. It does not have to do anything to be loved; its very being is enough to evoke warm feelings within most of us. So this need to be loved goes back to our origins, and how that need was met in our childhood will determine how good we are at relating to others when we grow up. In an ideal world the love and acceptance we receive in childhood will help us to cultivate a sense of self-esteem and value and give us an ability to give to others what has been given to us. But what if this love is not there in our history? Supposing we experience rejection, humiliation, abuse by others and an introjected sense of badness, what then? 'Love' will take on an entirely different meaning. We will spend most of our adult life looking for the love we never had in our childhood. For many this becomes a life-search, an odyssey, a searching for the Holy Grail.

Those who engage in this odyssey are looking for someone to supply the deficits of the past, and *this search is doomed to failure*. The awful truth is this: we can never have what we never had. But society has cultivated an awful lie to cover up this truth: 'You never grieve over what you never had!' On the contrary some of us spend our lives grieving (unconsciously) over the lost love of childhood. Ultimately we must come to the conclusion that lost love is *love lost*, irrecoverable. Our manic search for someone to make up for the deficit of love in our past is a cruel illusion. Grieving over such a loss is the most appropriate thing we can do with it. That is far more preferable to, and constructive than, projecting this need on to others to make up for what we never had in the past. Adult love can only be experienced at the adult level, never the child level that often we seek. The parent-baby marriages make sense but only as a pathetic caricature of lost child-love. 'What does my baby want? Does diddums want a cuddle then?' may be dismissed as playful intimacy but it contains within it too much truth for comfort. Such a pattern of relating gives rise to the doom-laden spectre of the Peter Pan and Wendy type of marriage.[41]

This basic need – to be loved – is, therefore, not as simple as it may at first appear. It makes our definition of love so much harder, for it can mean all kinds of things to different people, according to their personal histories. What appears a simple statement, 'You don't love me!' is far from simple. This statement can mean:

- Why don't you give me what I want?
- You don't understand me
- Meet my needs!
- Don't ask me for anything
- I am feeling abandoned
- Why are you never here when I need you?
- Treat me as a hungry baby! Feed me!
- Please don't get angry with me
- You must never criticize me
- My needs are more important than yours!

With such a confusion of potential messages within it, no wonder we find it hard to make a sensible response. One adult response would be, 'Tell me about your expectations of me', and put the onus on the questioner to define his or her terms.

Yet, supposing we have uncovered and grieved over childhood deficits of love, what then? Certain changes then follow:

1. We stop seeing others as potential *parents*
2. We stop seeing ourselves as a needy *child*
3. We start seeing ourselves and others as *adults*
4. We abandon our infantile odyssey for the long-lost love
5. We begin to realize the difference between 'need-love' (which comes from the empty heart) and 'gift-love' (which comes from the overflowing heart).

Armed with this knowledge and this experience of change, we are more fitted to engage in intimate relationships than ever in the past. The risk to love becomes more manageable precisely because *less hangs upon it*. We are seeking love and wanting to share love not because of the needs arising out of our Being, but out of our well-being. We seek love not in order to exist but in order to live joyfully. Once we know, through our love of self, that we exist, we seek the other for the fullest expression that it is *good* for us to exist. We come to the loved one in order to share what we have found about ourselves, and in order to enhance both them and us. We now have something to give, to share, and we want that something to grow and mature, together.

A new partner?
It is understandable when we hear others say to us, 'Never again!' Yet according to the latest figures available, each year about a quarter of a million people remarry.[42] Some of the reasons for this phenomenon have been examined above, and not all the motives are pure. Many people simply believe that they cannot live alone and take the first train that comes along. One gifted woman I know made such a choice several years ago, in the face of much confrontation by her friends. 'Well, at my age one can't

pick and choose,' she said. I reinforced the idea that age had little to do with her choice, and yet she married in haste and today repents at leisure.

There are many others, however, who have come through these phases of leavetaking successfully and have good and creative second marriages. There *is* life after divorce!

But are there discernible principles upon which we can base this success? I would offer the following check-list for your consideration if you are contemplating a second marriage:

- Finish your unfinished business with your former marriage
- Find out what Left Luggage you are still carrying, and let it go
- Let go of any bitterness, anger and resentment you feel towards your former spouse; forgive!
- Fulfil all your obligations towards your 'ex', especially financial ones
- Develop a wide network of support and encouragement
- Realize that you are more 'marketable' than you think
- Allow yourself to experiment with a number of relationships before opting for one
- Be bold in your honest expression of what you want out of a second marriage
- Find out how your intended new partner feels about your children (if any)
- If this is also your new partner's second marriage, check out how far he or she has processed their separation and divorce
- Establish new mutual ground rules for the proposed marriage.

Choosing a second partner is, naturally, a very personal

issue and depends upon so many variables that no one can tell you what to do and whom to choose. Yet there is still some truth to the old adage, 'The onlooker sees most!' and the advice of friends whose opinion you trust could be a great asset to you in your decision-making. It can be an exciting and life-enhancing time for you, and hopefully some of the warnings and encouragements above will make your journey more successful.

9. A New Life – For Me?

Carola Mann, a psychoanalyst and midlife researcher, has written of a movement across the midlife years from 'us-ness to me-ness'. A movement from primary self-identification in terms of roles and relationships to a primary self-identification in terms of one's experience of oneself. This process, which Jung calls 'individuation', happens only through multiple experiences of separation and loss. It is movement into a responsible autonomy in which one takes one's signals from within and directs his life from his own centre.

(Robert A. Raines, *Going Home*)[43]

For several reasons this has not been an easy book for me to write. It has opened up for me my own leavetaking from a long-distance marriage but I have tried not to make my experiences the yardstick for all leavetakings.

In many ways my life today is richer than I could ever have imagined. In the dark days in Rugby I rarely (if ever) looked too far into the future. Frankly I couldn't see beyond my programme of studies in the United States of America. What they might lead to was beyond the limited resources of my imagination. Looking back, I am amazed at the way in which my life has changed.

But if I had stayed in my dead marriage, would these

creative changes have happened anyway? Am I not just reading history in a contrived way? I don't believe I am, for at least one major reason: in common with many people I found that personal growth and the permission to be myself were impossible within the constrictions of the former relationship. The new life I have today would not have 'happened anyway', since the prevailing conditions for personal growth were not only absent but actually prohibited. Only as I dared to extricate myself from the confines of a dead relationship did I gain the strength to become myself and, through pain, take responsibility for fulfilling my personal potential.

Yet, as I have dared to risk sharing with you, I am painfully aware that given the circumstances of your own life at this moment, you may want to shout at me, 'It's all right for you! You've made it!' I want you to know that I appreciate how it feels when your life is not all right, turned upside down, and everything appears black and threatening. I've been there.

If there is one message I would want to convey through this book it would be this: After the separation from your partner, whether through death or divorce, there lies before you the possibility of a new and rewarding life.

CASE HISTORY: PEGGY

The day on which the doctor told Peggy the results of tests on her husband Dennis, her world seemed to come to an end. As she walked away from the hospital, life went blank. Suddenly there was no future there any more. She received the news with a detachment and numbness which would eventually thaw and reveal all the rawness and pain that the impending death of a partner can hold. Dennis and Peggy had always shared everything, and somehow they managed to support one another until Dennis passed peacefully away in his sleep.

Peggy shut herself away for a while. Later she was to describe this period of her life as a living death: a twilight existence in which all meaning and purpose – even the will to live – seemed to be absent. But slowly she emerged from this half-life; friends and family gently encouraged her to join them in their leisure pursuits. Peggy discovered that she rather liked ten pin bowling! She'd never been before, and somehow (she joked) it was rather satisfying to hurl the bowl down the alley and hear all those skittles tumbling over. She had no idea that she had so much energy. Slowly Peggy began to realize other things that she had submerged in the interests of her relationship with Dennis. He was strictly a home bird, with a bit of gardening for fresh air. Peggy had to re-learn about out-side activities; in fact she had never noticed the bowling alley, erected in the past year right under the car park Dennis used regularly on their shopping trips; Dennis had never allowed Peg to drive the car, and now, after one or two early mishaps with the garden gate, she was in her element and her wheels became her symbol of freedom. Soon her friends and family began to complain that she was never at home when they called. Dennis was a veg-etarian; soon Peggy rediscovered her appetite for fillet steak.

Peg also discovered her inner longing to visit the Greek islands. Rather like Shirley Valentine, Peg had allowed her husband's wishes regarding holidays to predominate; but now, like Shirley, Peg began to dream:

> I know what I'd like to do, I'd like to drink a glass of wine in a country where the grape is grown. Sittin' by the sea. Lookin' at the sun. But 'he' won't go abroad. Well y'see, he gets jet lag when we go to the Isle of Man. An' I wouldn't mind – we go by boat.

We've been going for fifteen years – he still won't drink the tap water. He's that type, Joe . . . If he doesn't wanna go abroad, well that's up to him. But that shouldn't stop me goin'. If I want to.[44]

So to Greece Peg went. She would have agreed, truth to tell, that Dennis was a bit like Joe in some respects, except that Dennis had never been even to the Isle of Man. Then, right in the middle of the 'dream' – when she was enjoying the sea and the sun and a bottle of Mavrodaphne wine – wham! Peg was hit by a massive guilty conscience.

It came with an almost physical force one day, out of the blue. She was suddenly overwhelmed with feelings of guilt for enjoying herself. It was as if voices within her were accusing her of disrespect for Dennis. 'Fancy you going off and having a good time, and him not cold in his grave!' Although her Greek holiday came more than a year after Dennis's death, her dream suddenly became a nightmare. Accusing voices seemed to well up from within, questioning her right to self-fulfilment and pro-ducing fear and panic and guilt. She was obviously a bad woman; worse – she was acting as if Dennis had never existed. How *could* she?

What was happening to Peggy? In psychological terms, fundamental issues were arising for her which demanded her attention and resolution. These issues centred upon the differences between her roles as a married and a single woman. As a married woman she had surrendered (only it had never appeared to her like surrender) many of her own preferences and choices in the interests of the good of the marriage. Dennis had brought his own preferences with him into the marriage, and truth to tell these seem to have dominated the relationship. He was such a loving man, and shared so much with Peg that it did not appear to her a sacrifice. All the accommodations she made were given gladly as a token of her love for him. Subtly, of course, she had undermined her own integrity and self-love by not stating her own preferences, and it was this split that suddenly erupted within her feelings of guilt. Her guilt was an acquired guilt rather than real (in so far as she had done nothing wrong). In other words she had so programmed her life to meeting Dennis's needs that her own had taken a back seat. Then, when they emerged naturally after Dennis's death, they were so different from her former behaviour pattern that the collision of interests (hers v. Dennis's) produced the guilt.

For a while Peg experienced much confusion and disquiet. But slowly she came to realize that her new life was not costing Dennis anything; indeed for the first time she admitted that that relationship was finished and her duty done. She could finally give herself permission to fulfil her life by pursuing her own interests, free from the paralyzing guilt she had felt while on holiday in Corfu.

Of course, not all the family (especially Dennis's) saw it this way. Whispers began to reach her of their disapproval. Dark murmurings of 'disgraceful', 'selfish', and doubts about her sanity floated around for a while. Interestingly enough, some of these were coming from the very people who had been encouraging her to 'get out a bit more'. As she began to look closer at *their* relationships Peg noticed that many of them were locked into a similar pattern to that which she and Dennis had chosen. She discovered that some of them were actually motivated, not by care and concern for her but by envy. They were secretly wishing that they had some of the freedom that she was claiming for herself! And one way of dealing with that envy was to try and make Peg feel guilty.

Shirley Valentine's daughter Millandra expressed it this way: 'I think it's a disgrace . . . I think it's disgustin'.' Such is the built-in resistance to those who wish to discover a new life for themselves, as they struggle to find the 'good' in their 'goodbye'.

In their important book, *Second Chances*, the authors list among the psychological tasks of divorce 'Reclaiming oneself'. They write:

> This is another step that, along with mourning, signifies detachment from the marriage. It involves reclaiming or establishing a new sense of self, a new sense of identity. In a long-term marriage, a partner's sense of identity is tied to his or her spouse and to the marriage. . . . These roles fall away at divorce [or death] and a new sense of self needs to be built to replace the old identity.[45]

While not all of us will suffer the pangs of guilt that Peggy did, it will frequently occur in our breaking out period that we have to battle with the status quo, the way things were in our marriage. Our newly-won freedom – whether taken by us or given to us – contains almost limitless opportunities for self-fulfilment. Because the sadness or anger or relief of separation seems to occupy the foreground of our feelings for a while, they often hide the future 'good' that our 'goodbye' contains within it. What does that 'good' consist of?

I think there are at least three elements in the 'good' in 'goodbye':

(a) Freedom
(b) Growth
(c) Joy

Freedom

It is important that we keep before us the positive elements in our goodbyes. Of these, perhaps freedom is the most important. But if we think that this is simply stating the obvious, then read carefully the words of Erich Fromm, for your ability to enjoy your freedom may be affected by them:

> Is there not also, perhaps, besides an innate desire for freedom, an instinctive wish for submission? If there is not, how can we account for the attraction which submission to a leader has for so many to-day? Is submission always to an overt authority, or is there also submission to internalized authorities, such as duty or conscience, to inner compulsions or to anony-mous authorities like public opinion? Is there a hidden satisfaction in submitting, and what is its essence?[46]

This lure of submission – whether to the patterns of behaviour established in our previous marriage or to those inner voices (the 'internalized authorities') – is going to become a major stumbling-block on the road to our per-sonal freedom. For we are going to have to deal with the 'oughts', 'shoulds' and 'ought nots' if we are ever to break free from submission to our past. Many people interpret their role in marriage through the concept of submission – and this fits well with the psychological type of person known as the Pleaser. Their whole *raison d'être* within the marriage has been to meet the needs of their partner, and this role for obvious historical reasons, has largely been adopted by the woman. Such a position is found in *A Doll's House* by Henrik Ibsen. Torvald's wife Nora finally finds the courage to confront her husband:

> . . . You've always been so kind to me. But our home has been nothing but a play-room. I've been

your doll-wife here, just as at home I was Papa's doll-child. And the children have been my dolls in their turn. I liked it when you came and played with me, just as they liked it when I came and played with them. That's what our marriage has been, Torvald.

When eventually Nora decides to leave Torvald, he confronts her decision:

TORVALD   But this is disgraceful. Is this the way you neglect your most sacred duties?

NORA   What do you consider is my most sacred duty?

TORVALD   Do I have to tell you that? Isn't it your duty to your husband and children?

NORA   I have another duty, just as sacred.

TORVALD   You can't have. What duty do you mean?

NORA   My duty to myself.[47]

Of course, there are those 'rolling-pin' marriages where the hen-pecked husband has either chosen the submissive role or had it thrust upon him by *force majeure*. But where this pattern of behaviour can be discerned, then the submissive role within the partnership has been the dominant one, and to such people the concept of freedom can appear both strange and threatening.

In many cases the submissive partner will simply look round for another dominant partner to fasten on to, and so the neurotic pattern will be repeated. Interestingly enough, an example of this pattern of behaviour was presented within a counselling session that occurred at the time I was writing the above paragraph. An attractive young lady was finding it difficult to confront her partner and did not want to burden him with her problems. When I suggested we looked at her history to find out where she had learned that way of relating, she immediately remembered that when she was thirteen her mother and father went through a severe matrimonial trauma, and it hadn't seemed fair to my client to 'burden' her mother when she had enough troubles of her own. She was amazed to find that, twenty years later, she was still locked into that way of regarding whatever she wanted to share with her partner as a burden to him, and that she still discounted the importance of her own problems. What this young woman discovered was that she was subtly discounting her own needs and at the same time taking responsibility for the feelings of her partner. 'Not wanting to upset him' was a form of submission. It was also a form of self-protection, as all forms of protection must be, to some extent.

So freedom is not always the easy option it may seem. In order to exercise it, we have to overcome the stumbling-blocks erected in our past, and particularly in the past marriage. Here is a check-list for you to work through at your leisure:

A freedom-lover's charter

- In setting myself free from my previous relationship I need lose nothing of what was good and loving
- When my marriage broke down, the mould in which I was contained broke at the same time
- A mould can contain and make me feel safe, but it also limits my freedom
- I have within me a creator, a potter, who can create a new way of defining who I am
- I am free to decide who I am and who I want to become
- Can I dare to let go of the security of those things that bound me to my former partner?

- There is much more to the real me than was ever shown in my past relationship
- How did I come to feel ashamed of the real me, and how did I collude in fashioning my own limitations?
- Freedom is expanding my personal, social and spiritual boundaries to meet my own contemporary needs
- Doing what I want to do is not being selfish – it is affirming my own value and power
- Because I never learned to love myself, I was over-dependent on the love of other people
- When I take the risk of loving myself, I am free from dependency and more open to be loved by others
- Freedom is taking responsibility for myself and my own happiness and not blaming others for my misery
- My needs are just as important as anyone else's; I don't have to fall into the old trap of putting everyone else first
- Who taught me that I was worthless, helpless, valueless? Can I dare to believe that they were wrong?
- What scares me most about freedom? Is it that I have become overdependent upon the approval of others?
- When I am overdependent upon the approval of others I become submissive and throw away my personal freedom
- There is no law of the universe that says that something cannot happen for the first time!
- Freedom is giving myself permission to choose
- I may make mistakes, but I am responsible for them
- I am free to abandon my need to be perfect

- I am free to abandon my old compulsive habit of always meeting the expectations of others
- I must take responsibility for my slavery
- When I honour my own freedom, I also honour that of other people; I need neither manipulate nor enslave them.

Growth

Without freedom it is impossible to grow.

As human beings we have within us an almost limitless ability to grow and develop in all kinds of ways. What prevents us from seeing this is often found in the limiting factors in our past history: parents and parental figures, religious and educational teachers and our peer groupings. Stale and dead marriages are notorious breeding grounds for the restriction of our growth.

What we need to begin with, of course, is a dynamic – rather than a static – view of life itself. It is so easy to fall into the mistaken assumptions that life is planned out for us, it's all written in the stars, and whatever others dish out to us in our marriage is both inevitable and probably no more than what we deserve.

This is utterly self-defeating. There can be no personal growth while we suffer from such delusions. We all know of marriages in which it is plain that one of the partners is being held back, or as Shakespeare described it, 'cabined, cribbed, confined' (*Macbeth* III. iv. 24). Such restrictions are very frequently found to be sexist in origin, some fragile male ego held together by the sacrifices of his intellectually superior wife. Jealous tantrums by him can be obviated only by the submission of her; the price of the marriage staying viable depends on the concessions she is expected to make. She is asked to make the choice between her advancing career and her marriage. On such choices many marriages flounder, when the wife decides that enough is enough. She decides to break out of the suffocating atmosphere of the marriage, risking family cries of 'selfish', and decides to become her own person. Here is the dynamic approach in action, but of course many partners never make that choice. They stay in the marriage for all kinds of reasons and mould their lives within the strict limitations of their partner's expectations. They moulder and decay. Some crumb of comfort may be snatched at through believing that their sacrifices are keeping the marriage intact ('for the sake of the children' and the fear of 'being selfish') but usually such crumbs are not enough to survive within the marriage.

Growing means changing

That can be a very frightening thing for those people who have never discovered their potential. Old habits of self-denial and self-effacement seem to die hard. But after we have worked our way through the four phases of leavetaking we are in a better position to make very positive choices about our future. Once we have overcome the temptation to start a passionate relationship with the first person that comes along or, alternatively, overcome the avowed intention of never having anything to do with anyone of the opposite sex, we can see more clearly that there is a great deal of choice between these two extremes. There is, for instance, the cultivation of a wide circle of friends, including those of the opposite sex, who can broaden our horizons and interests. It is within this circle of friends that we can experiment with new opportunities, new choices and new risks. To use a shopping metaphor, instead of making for the cornflakes, we can take our time looking along the whole shelf to see what is on offer. If we find we don't like muesli, we have at least made a discovery, and need not repeat it. But the important thing

is that we have broken out of our old habit of thinking
that the only breakfast cereal is cornflakes and we will
never adopt that attitude again. Once we have seen the
complete range of cereals we cannot unknow that fact.
Similarly in our new and exciting relationships we are free
to make different choices, changing our old predictable
habits of the way in which we have viewed ourselves (and
others) and daring to make creative changes which will
enrich our lives.

Joy

This is the third element of the 'good' in 'goodbye'. I
mention it specifically since many people in the throes of
divorce believe that they will never be happy again. With
the departure of their spouse they come to the conclusion
that happiness has departed with them. For a while this
may feel to be true, especially in the early phases of leavetaking. There may indeed be more misery than happiness
around in those early days, but as we work our way
through to the future phase there is a vast potential for
breaking through to a new experience of love and joy.
This is how Mel Krantzler found it:

> After our remarriage shock subsided, Pat and I were
> to experience many other surprises as we settled 'up'
> to married life. In the past, marriage has been
> described as the time for settling 'down'. Settling
> down implies restricting personal growth, limiting
> individual possibilities. Old-style marriage was the
> way one proved oneself a socially accepted adult.
> Each partner assumed preordained marital roles and
> obligations: king-of-the-Castle husband who was also
> the provider and responsible father; deferential wife
> who was also the nest builder, sex receptacle, and

mother. They pledged togetherness till the end of time even though time might erode all dreams, hopes, and expectations. No, Pat and I had no intention of settling 'down' to married life. We, along with millions of other divorced people, are fortunate to be living in a world that allows men and women to explore different options for themselves.[48]

Mel and Pat had rediscovered the joy of intimacy. Of course, it means risk-taking – even taking the risk that we will be hurt again – but if we have overcome our earlier beliefs that we were powerless, helpless and defenceless, then we can take those risks in a calculated way. This may mean not allowing ourselves to be rushed into precipitate decisions we may regret. This will apply especially in the important area of new sexual relationships.

Like much else in leavetaking, opinions about sexual activity with new partners will vary widely. The variables will depend upon upbringing, religious affiliation (if any) and personal ethics. In this important period of change we may choose to review our moral attitudes in order to discover where we got them from in the first place. Are we merely mouthing what our mother (or grandmother) taught us, or have we ever made up our own minds about the rights and wrongs of sex? Since it is likely in some cases that our first marriage took place in the pre-AIDS period, we may never have had to think about the question of safe sex; or you may have been introduced to these questions by your former partner's 'sleeping around' and the possibility that they may have contracted the disease. Either way, in any serious relationship this will be something you will want to discuss with a future sexual partner; and you will take precautions (or professional advice) accordingly.

The joy of sex is one of the most exciting discoveries

that we can ever make (Dr Alex Comfort's *The Joy of Sex* is a useful place to start if you want a general introduction to the subject). In spite of the cultural revolution of the 1960s there is still a large amount of ignorance and taboo about sex. Nowhere in the repertoire of human behaviour are there more hang-ups, let-downs and general rubbish talked about than on the subject of sex. Historically we carry a huge amount of guilt and we will need to take a careful look at what happened sexually within our former marriage in order to find out what were the prevailing patterns and assumptions. We certainly don't have to take those as sacrosanct. We are free to change, try new and daring experiments and not immediately suppose that a new sexual partner who enjoys oral sex is obviously a pervert! Try it. If you don't like something, you're free to say no. It's all right to express your own preferences and, within the context of love, seek and give mutual understanding.

The joy of sex, however, is only one of the many joys that await us in a new relationship. Companionship, security, sharing, being listened to, having fun – all these joys and others besides are among the exciting discoveries awaiting us in the fullness of the future. Ending a relationship can truly feel like the end of the world; yet it also holds within it all the vast opportunities of creating a new one. There is life after death or divorce. It is simply up to us to reach out and make it happen.

Notes

1. *Couples Arguing: Guidelines to Effective Communication* (1987); *Couples in Counselling: A Consumer's Guide to Marriage Counselling* (1989); *Couples Growing: A Companions' Guide to Long Distance Marriage* (1991).
2. Sam Keen, *The Passionate Life* (Gateway, 1985), p. 32.
3. 'Let's Hang On' (new edn Crewe/Randell/Linzer, Telstar Records Ltd, 1988).
4. William Bridges, *Transitions* (Addison-Wesley, 1980), p. 109f.
5. Sam Keen, *To a Dancing God* (Fontana, 1970), p. 1.
6. C. S. Lewis, *A Grief Observed* (Faber, 1966), p. 7.
7. Woody Allen, *Without Feathers*, Sphere, 1978.
8. Rainer Maria Rilke, *Letters to a Young Poet* (W. W. Norton, 1934), p. 35.
9. Robert A. Raines, *Going Home* (Harper & Row, 1979), p. 30.
10. ibid., p. 48.
11. I gratefully acknowledge thanks to John C. Haskey's important article, 'Grounds for Divorce in England and Wales: a Social and Demographic Analysis', *Journal of Biosocial Sciences*, 18 (1986), pp. 127–53, in this section.
12. Jack Dominian, *Marital Breakdown* (Pelican, 1968), p. 42.
13. Harville Hendrix, *Getting the Love You Want* (Harper & Row, 1990), p. 14.
14. Dominian, p. 62.
15. ibid. p. 66f, my italics.
16. quoted in ibid. p. 79f.
17. A. Alvarez, *Life after Marriage* (1982), quoted in *The Oxford Book of Marriage*.
18. Susan Jeffers, *Opening Our Hearts to Men* (Piatkus, 1989), p. 261f.
19. Hendrix, op. cit. p. 110.
20. See further, Jordan and Margaret Paul, *Do I Have to Give Up ME to be Loved by YOU?* (Grapevine, 1988).

21. Christopher Clulow and Janet Mattinson, *Marriage Inside Out* (Penguin, 1989), p. 145.
22. Phillip Hodson, *Observer Sunday*, 25 February 1990.
23. Willy Russell, *Shirley Valentine* (Methuen, 1989), p. 14f.
24. *The Myths of Greece and Rome* (Harrap, 1908), p. 16.
25. George Bernard Shaw, *Getting Married* (Penguin, 1986), p. 135.
26. Judith S. Wallerstein and Sandra Blakeslee, *Second Chances* (Corgi, 1990), p. 321.
27. *Today*, 18 November 1988.
28. M. Scott Peck, *The Road Less Travelled* (Touchstone, 1978), p. 145.
29. ibid.
30. Madonna Kolbenschlag, *Kiss Sleeping Beauty Goodbye* (Harper & Row, 1988), p. 127.
31. *Couples in Counselling*, p. 14f.
32. Henri Nouwen, *The Living Reminder* (Seabury, 1977), p. 44.
33. Raines, op. cit. p. 44.
34. Paul Tillich, quoted in Sam Keen, *Beginnings Without End* (Harper & Row, 1977), p. 52.
35. Mel Krantzler, *Creative Divorce* (Signet, 1974).
36. Scott Peck, op. cit. p. 30.
37. Bridges, op. cit. p. 130.
38. Jordan and Margaret Paul, op. cit. p. 3.
39. Anaïs Nin in Mel Krantzler, *Learning to Love Again* (Harper & Row, 1977), p. 51.
40. ibid.
41. see *Couples Growing*, p. 40.
42. ibid. p. 131.
43. Raines, op. cit. p. 42.
44. Russell, op. cit. p. 4.
45. Wallerstein and Blakeslee, op. cit. p. 321f.
46. Erich Fromm, *The Fear of Freedom* (Ark, 1985), p. 4.
47. Henrik Ibsen, *A Doll's House* (Penguin, 1965), pp. 227–8.
48. Krantzler, *Learning to Love Again*, op. cit. p. 193f.

Further Reading

Going Home, Robert A. Raines (Harper & Row, 1979)

Second Chances, Judith S. Wallerstein and Sandra Blakeslee (Corgi, 1990)

Learning to Love Again, Mel Krantzler (Harper & Row, 1977)

Do I have to Give Up ME to be Loved by YOU? Jordan and Margaret Paul (Grapevine, 1987)

Uncoupling, Diane Vaughan (Methuen, 1987)

Parting: The Aftermath of Separation and Divorce, Graham B. Spanier and Linda Thompson (Sage, 1987)

Marital Breakdown, Jack Dominian (Penguin, 1971)

Shirley Valentine, Willy Russell (Methuen, 1989)

Living Together, Feeling Alone, Dan Kiley (Cedar, 1991)

The Joy of Sex (new rev. edn 1991)

The Single Experience, Keith and Andrea Wells Miller (Word Books, 1980)

Helping Children Cope with Divorce, Rosemary Wells (Sheldon Press, 1989)

Mike's Lonely Summer: A Child's Guide through Divorce, Carolyn Nystrom (Lion Books, 1986)

Index

Organic,
I N C.